CITIES AND SCHOOLS
in the
GILDED AGE

Kennikat Press
National University Publications
Interdisciplinary Urban Studies

General Editor

Raymond A. Mohl
Florida Atlantic University

William A. Bullough

CITIES AND SCHOOLS
in the
GILDED AGE

THE EVOLUTION OF
AN URBAN INSTITUTION

National University Publications
KENNIKAT PRESS • 1974
Port Washington, N. Y. • London

Manufactured in the United States of America

Published by
Kennikat Press Corp.
Port Washington, N.Y./London

Library of Congress Cataloging in Publication Data

Bullough, William A.　　　1933-
　　Cities and schools in the gilded age.

　　(Interdisciplinary urban studies) (National univer-
sity publications)
　　Includes bibliographical references and index.
　　1. Education, Urban - - United States - - History.
I.　Title.
LC5131.B84　　　　370.19'348'0973　　　74-80592
ISBN 0-8046-9094-4

For my father
who would have been pleased
and for my mother, for my wife, and
for my son

Contents

Acknowledgments

No individual writes a book, and merely listing all who have had a part in producing mine would require a second volume. However, much more than academic courtesy mandates the recognition of at least a few.

First among these is Professor Alexander B. Callow, Jr., of the University of California at Santa Barbara, a unique mentor and superb friend. His consistently enthusiastic, frequently demanding, and constantly penetrating guidance of the initial study has contributed a major portion of whatever merit the work may have.

Two other scholars must also be recognized: Professor Otey M. Scruggs of Syracuse University, who sowed the seed, and Professor David B. Tyack of Stanford University, who shared his time, his resources, and his interest.

For intellectual stimulation and congenial friendship, my warmest appreciation goes to my colleagues in the Department of History at California State University, Hayward. Among them, I owe particular thanks to Professors José A. Fernández-Santamaría, Gerald S. Henig, and Richard J. Orsi, for time and energy freely given and for instructive criticism.

I must also recognize numerous colleagues and multitudes of students who shared my years as a public school teacher. Together we endured the vicissitudes of the reformers' "system," and the experience helped to prompt the writing of this book.

Finally, for those to whom the work is dedicated and for all whose names cannot appear here but should, I have but two words: thank you. I hope you all know how much they mean.

W. A. B.

Fremont, California
September 1974

CITIES AND SCHOOLS
in the
GILDED AGE

Introduction:

Americans and Their Schools

> *The very spring and root of honesty and virtue*
> *lie in the felicity of lighting on good education.*
> —Plutarch

A Frenchman, visiting the United States in 1895, observed that "the indispensible [sic] corollary to the study of the life of a people is the study of its educational processes."[1] Such an assertion, perhaps, has special—though not exclusive—validity when the people studied is that of the United States. From earliest colonial times, Americans have registered an abiding commitment to education as an instrument of progress. That commitment, however, has been less than consistent both in conceptualization of methods and purposes and in public receptivity and support.

In general, American attitudes and expectations regarding education have been closely tied to major social, political, and economic developments and to the needs of society. Moreover, despite a rhetoric thoroughly democratic and idealistic in tone, education in the United States has been, with rare exception, utilitarian in conception and practice. English colonists, for example, understood education as the conservator of civilization in the midst of a savage and hostile wilderness. Later Americans defined it as a preparation for the unexpected in a socially and economically fluid society, and later still, they conceived it as a prerequisite for maintaining republican institutions.[2] Education, too, has been responsive—as in the Jacksonian Era

3

under the leadership of Horace Mann and Henry Barnard—
to significant historical trends such as expanding suffrage.

It should not be assumed, however, that responsiveness
has always manifested itself in thoroughgoing reforms within
the educational system itself or consisted of an intensified
popular commitment to free and formal public education.
Indeed, many of the Jacksonians who accepted education as
a necessity of democracy were simultaneously suspicious of
anything that savored of intellectualism or academic privilege.[3]
Furthermore, a prominent tenet of the American faith in education has been a confidence in informal or self-education
derived through the application of formal education and common sense to experience in order to increase knowledge and
practical skill. That confidence, coupled with the assumption
that the benefits of such informal education have constantly
been equally within the reach of all, has not infrequently operated to reduce popular commitment to and support for public
education.

Nor should it be assumed that American education has
been closely integrated with changes in society. Although it
has been suggested that the ideal of public education has consistently embodied the Platonic concept of education for the
good life and the good society, formal education has acted
more as an instrument for the preservation of the status quo
than as a vehicle for social change. Indeed, Horace Mann's
often quoted definition of education as "the balance-wheel of
the social machinery" has proved in practice even more appropriate than Mann anticipated. Despite the consistently articulated commitment to individualism which has permeated
American pedagogical rhetoric, educational practice has demonstrated an equally consistent effort to mold the individual to
society's conception of the good citizen, whether or not that
pattern was entirely relevant to the individual's experience or
environment. Ironically, this has been the case even in attempts
at compensatory education such as the effort on behalf of the
freedmen during Radical Reconstruction, the development of
the kindergarten and the manual training movement in the

last quarter of the nineteenth century, or the attempt to "Americanize" the immigrant early in the twentieth century.[4]

Although educators and institutions have demonstrated awareness of changes occurring in society and of the necessity for the school to respond to those changes, their reactions have generally been ambivalent, peripheral, and incomplete. They have been based less upon understandings of new social and economic realities than upon commitments to the values of the past and often to outmoded conceptions of society itself. It might even be asserted that American educational institutions, despite their definition as agencies of progress, have been, in fact, among the least progressive of American institutions, tending more toward the preservation of ideals and values of an earlier period than toward promoting social innovation, adaptation to the present, or preparation for the future. The condition is, to be sure, illustrative of problems inherent in all popularly controlled institutions in a majoritarian society when altered conditions create needs not synonymous with those of the majority or the presumed spokesmen for the majority. But more than this, the failure of education to be more than an "imperfect panacea," despite continuing American faith in its efficacy, raises numerous important questions.[5]

How, for example, can academicians and educational administrators in large cities—often physically, socially, and economically detached from the masses for whose education they have been made responsible—discover the realities of the educational needs of those masses? How, once those requirements are identified, may they be translated into positive educational programs in the public schools? Moreover, even when needs are actually known and positive programs devised, is the public school the appropriate agency through which to act? Or do changing conditions demand alternative and more adaptable institutions to achieve results traditionally sought through the public schools? Finally, assuming that the limitations of public education are recognized and relevant programs defined, how may popular moral and economic support be secured for what certainly must be expensive and possibly even radical educational innovations?

Specific answers to such questions should not be anticipated from an investigation of the past; for the task of supplying them lies more within the provinces of educators and sociologists than within those of historians. Nevertheless, an institutional study of the development of urban school systems in the last quarter of the nineteenth century may shed some light upon the realities of the American educational experience and have some relevance for current educational concerns. There are hazards involved in searching for parallels in history, but in the last quarter of the twentieth century the urban school is among the most critical of educational concerns. And the general outlines of the problem in many ways resemble those of the dilemma faced by educators in the Gilded Age. Indeed, modern urban educational systems are essentially the result of attempts to cope with that dilemma. Moreover, although attention is currently focused upon the educational conditions of inner city schools, even the more affluent suburbs are becoming increasingly involved in the debate. Not only have fiscal problems, the question of local control, and the dilemma of achieving racial—no longer ethnic—balance in individual schools aroused the attention of both urban and suburban sectors, but concern for the relevance of educational programs and institutions also has become increasingly audible, insistent, and even strident. Finally, as in the late 1800s, the entire question of the public schools has become intensely political.

Current concern leaves little doubt that Americans continue to take their schools seriously or that their criticism is the product of genuine solicitude. Indeed, in this they remain strictly within the historical tradition of placing intensive emphasis upon the importance of education and, in many cases, ranking it with home, church, and state as an elemental institution of civilized society. It might even be argued that Americans have regarded the school as the primary institution, the molder and conservator of other institutions. Such a concept has been a dominant theme not only among educators but also among laymen, and it formed a significant facet of Gilded Age educational thought. One Cleveland educator articulated the understanding of many of her colleagues—and of many of her countrymen before and since—when she addressed the National Education Association (NEA) convention in 1889. Although she acknowledged the fact that the vast majority of American children left school before their twelfth birthday and that most received only four years of formal education, she also expected amazing results. Her expectations were typical.

The school life, brief as it is, may reasonably be asked to furnish to the Republic loyal and obedient citizens; to the business world, men with a courage and a grip that will not too easily let go in the pushing affairs of trade; to social life, an ease and grace of manners, a strength of self-reliance, which shall put each in possession of his full powers for his own up-building and for the advancement of his associates; and *to the home life of the nation,* men and women pure in heart, clear in conviction, strong in purpose, loving their children and loving to live with them.[6]

Such was the American faith in the common school.

Although Americans have expected much from their educational institutions—indeed, perhaps *because* they have expected much—they have rarely been satisfied. A boundless faith in education has inhibited, and often continues to inhibit, the institution's adaptibility and consequently its effectiveness. The faith has bred a species of educational Pollyannaism evident not only in popular attitudes but also in those of professional educators and historians of American education. Commitment to traditional education as a universal remedy has led many into the trap Voltaire described as a "mania for declaring when things are going badly that all is well," and to overlook the possibility that the cure-all they prescribed has been hardly more than a placebo. Historians of education have been afflicted with abundant optimism, until recent years perpetuating the idea that the American school system has represented a continuum of progress from the colonial dame school to the modern educational institution. The unfortunate results of the tendency to write educational history on the basis of the exception or the ideal—Horace Mann's crusade for the common school, Francis Wayland Parker's experiments at Quincy, or John Dewey's innovations in Chicago—rather than the realities of practice in the average classroom have been twofold: the assumption that all was indeed well, and a reticence to change.[7]

Because of such optimistic attitudes, many problems which might have been solved by more malleable institutions—or alternative institutions—constitute the heritage of succeeding generations. And because many of the urban institutions which confront the current crises in city schools are legacies of the Gilded Age—an era when cities became a preeminent feature of the American landscape—the development of common school systems in the late nineteenth-century city, and the ideologies that defined that development, provide particularly significant subjects for historical investigation. Although the changes that occurred in the American city of the Gilded Age were rapid and often radical, it is clear that educators were aware of such physical transformations and their social implications for the school. Indeed, as early as 1874 two leading educators defined the changes and, in their own terms, the impact of those changes on the public school.

In order to compensate for the lack of family-nurture [resulting from urbanization], the school is obliged to lay more stress upon discipline and to make far more prominent the moral phase of education. It is obliged to train pupils into habits of prompt obedience to his teachers and the practice of self-control in its various forms, in order that he may be prepared for a life wherein there is little police-restraint on the part of constituted authorities.[8]

It is a revealing comment, not only in terms of limitations of late nineteenth-century definitions of education but also in terms of educators' awareness that the city was making important changes in the nature of American life. A quarter century later, John Dewey defined the educational implications of urbanization much more comprehensively:

population is hurriedly gathered into cities from the ends of the earth; habits of living are altered with startling abruptness and thoroughness; the search for truths of nature is infinitely stimulated and facilitated and their application to life made not only practicable, but commercially necessary. Even our moral and religious ideas and interests . . . are profoundly affected.

Dewey recognized that urbanization had made important changes in American life and that the school had a significant role to play in adjusting or replacing the institutions—the family, the church, the workshop—that formerly supplied vital social, moral, and economic understandings in preurban society. A decade later, another eminent educator, Ellwood P. Cubberly, reaffirmed concern for the impact of urbanization: "In the cities, towns, and newer portions of the country these old educative influences and traditions have largely broken down, or have entirely ceased to exist." And he was confident that the school could and would replace them.[9]

Despite the persistence and breadth of such remarks and many more like them, educators and educational reformers, in their effort to adjust the schools to conform to new urban conditions, more often defined education as an agency of control than as one of change, and reform focused more upon structural reorganization than upon altering the basic concepts of education in keeping with novel conditions. But more than this, as even the progressive Dewey's comment reveals, the goal of reform remained essentially retrospective, premised upon attitudes derived from an earlier stage of social organization. And the outlooks that molded urban school reform went well beyond definitions of the function of education to include judgments about society, the state, politics, and even the city itself.[10]

Because of these varied influences, it may be misleading to allude to the effort to reform urban schools in the Gilded Age as a movement, for no national organization analogous to the National Municipal League or the League of American Municipalities coordinated the endeavor. Yet through the National Education Association—and particularly through that organization's Department of Superintendence—there developed a nationwide consensus regarding the nature of good urban schools, their organization, and their function. Indeed, in many of its particulars that consensus was similar to the ideology, style, and practice of concurrent municipal reform. Moreover, on occasion the same individuals involved themselves in both educational and municipal reform, and school reorganization often constituted an integral part of municipal charter revision drives. Finally, the specific goals of municipal and educational reform involved strong similarities: efficiency, centralization, expertise, civil service, bureaucratic organization, and nonpartisanship. Beyond the conditions that motivated them, the nature of their ideologies, and the character of their remedies, the two movements also embodied similar responses to the changing social, political, and economic milieu of the Gilded Age and to its intellectual climate. And, as turn-of-the-century municipal reform established structural patterns that have become standard in the political organization of American cities, so too have the systems evolved by educational reformers of the same era—for good or ill—provided the accepted modes of modern city school organization.

In the Gilded Age, however, these systems were limited in scope, involving mainly the elementary grades. For it was only at this level, known as the "common school," that universal education was approached in the nineteenth century. Though the expansion of the high school has been an important corollary of urbanization, public secondary schools in 1900 enrolled less than 1 percent of the nation's population. Therefore, the development of the public high school is most properly understood as a twentieth-century phenomenon.[11] Indeed, not until the period following World War I did the high school begin to replace the common school as the standard of educational achievement. For most nineteenth-century Americans, the lower grades remained the ultimate in educational expectations, and it was the institution through which educational progress might be attained. Moreover, despite vigorous efforts to extend the length of time children remained in school—in terms of both the length of the school year and the number of years of study—the common school remained the principal agency through which educators, reformers, politicians, and private citizens alike expected to secure adjustment —or conformity—to a changing urban environment.

It was an inherently limited institution, usually consisting of the first eight grades and occasionally one more grade at the upper level or a kindergarten at the lower. Nevertheless, the urban common school was expected to replace or restore the sense of community that had existed in the village as well as the family ties broken by the physical, social, and economic conditions of urban life, the political harmony that had supposedly existed in preurban society, and even the vocational training that had been an integral part of the rural experience. Further, the common school, defined as "the one central institution which presents to each the means of freedom" and as a microcosm of the "infant republic," was presumed to be not only the source of general literacy but also a common ground upon which all classes could meet and learn to live in harmony.[12]

Because it was the universal educational institution in the Gilded Age city, educators focused their attention on the common school, and what they said and wrote about it in the late 1800s provides a rich mine of raw material for the historical study of the attitudes that shaped urban school institutions. In the yearly publications of the NEA, in the *Annual Reports* and other publications of the U.S. Bureau of Education, in books and professional journals, and in numerous periodicals, educators poured out their ideas, opinions, and intentions. They discoursed upon academic, social, and economic functions of the school, upon its purposes, and upon its organization. And educators were sufficiently articulate, prolific, and consistent to leave little doubt concerning their basic ideas and attitudes or the sincerity of their commitment. Despite tendencies to define goals and assess results on the basis of personal values and preconceptions rather than social and economic realities, educators were honest enough to leave a clear record of both ideological and practical aspects of urban educational reform in the Gilded Age.

On the basis of that evidence, however, it is difficult to argue with the conclusion of one recent historian.

We must face the painful fact that this country has never, on any large scale, known vital urban schools, ones which embrace and are embraced by the mass of the community, which formulate their goals in terms of the individual instead of the fear of social dynamite or the imperatives of economic growth.[13]

Why that assessment has validity not only for the Gilded Age, a period of dynamic urban growth in the history of the United States, but also for American society nearly a century later is a question of crucial importance.

Some answers are apparent. Spectacular urbanization characterized the Gilded Age. Cities grew in number and size at unprecedented rates, and concurrent industrialization and in-migrations of formerly nonurban populations only served to heighten the problems of growth. Moreover, urban leaders— whether educators, reformers, or politicians—lacked models for the institutions they were called upon to develop in the burgeoning cities. The process of urbanization itself also complicated the problem by fragmenting traditional institutions of social cohesion. New conditions impaired the function of the home as a social and educational unit, the influence of the church upon major segments of the population diminished, and shifting economic relationships called many traditional assumptions into question.

However, numerous more subtle and potentially more significant impediments to effective school reform must also be considered. Well before the turn of the century, influenced by innovations in transportation technology, the process of suburbanization had already begun to divide communities physically, to separate classes, and to shift political balances and interests. Habits of thought inherited from the rural-agrarian past, no longer valid bases for judgment and action, continued to exert substantial influence on the process of urban decision making. Similarly, intellectual trends including Darwinian and Spencerian thought, the influence of business and industry upon ideas, and a growing commitment to organization, rationalization, and efficiency all influenced the development of the urban school—not only through their prestige among educational policy makers but also through their acceptance by substantial elements of the urban decision-making public. Indeed, educational reform in the Gilded Age frequently embodied a negative quality, an attack upon symptoms of chaos in American society and an effort to establish order through organization, centralization, and bureaucracy. Ironically, the result of that effort has been the perpetuation not only of the positive consequences of reform but also of its less commendable tendencies toward rigidity.[14]

Schools in American cities may yet be paying the price for the successes of turn-of-the-century reform. The highly structured educational systems which emerged from that period remain essentially intact, increasing the difficulty of evolving programs and institutions relevant to the demands and needs of a constantly changing urban society and frequently impeding the flow of communication between the schools themselves and the public they serve. If educational institutions are to be effective instruments for creating a more amenable urban environment, if they are to be "public" in the sense of democratic, if they are to be what Americans have traditionally expected them to be, and if the mistakes of the past are to be avoided, a thorough understanding of the evolution of now familiar institutions is imperative.

1

Urban Children and City Schools:

The Challenge of Numbers

> *It was in making education not only common to all, but in some sense compulsory on all, that the destiny of the free republics of America was practically settled.*
>
> —James Russell Lowell

Urbanization and industrialization in the last quarter of the nineteenth century subjected the United States to radical changes which modified economic practices, redefined political processes and institutions, drastically altered traditional relationships, and confronted public education with one of the most serious challenges in its history. Neither the rise of the city nor its implications were unnoticed by professional educators. Indeed, even though census data would confirm the numerical dominance of the urban population only in 1920, an official of the U.S. Bureau of Education recognized the growing breadth of the city's influence on all aspects of American life—including the school—a generation earlier when he observed that "the influence of cities in determining the general welfare [of the nation] is out of all proportion beyond the numbers of their population." The statement's overall accuracy in 1885, when state capitals still dominated urban affairs, may be subject to qualification. Still, it indicates clearly that educators, even at the national level, recognized the country's progress toward becoming an urban nation, a process accelerated by innovations in efficient transportation and communication. However, not the nationwide impact of the city but the specific practical implications of the new environment constituted the initial primary concerns of urban educators, and demographic changes confronted them with the most apparent problems. They observed that the lure of the city attracted immigrants from Europe and migrants from the American countryside and that the newcomers' children strained the capacity of already crowded city schools to accommodate them. And they recognized that numerical growth and urbanization severely challenged traditional assumptions, goals, and ideals of public education. Indeed, by 1881 Commissioner of Education John Eaton had defined difficulties arising from urban expansion—insufficient classrooms and teachers, increasing truancy and absenteeism, inappropriate curriculum and methodology, inadequate sanitary facilities, and organizational and administrative structures incapable of responding to novel conditions—as the most pressing concerns of American public education.[1]

Eaton was correct, of course. For even if numerous intangible problems related to newcomers are disregarded— their unfamiliarity with urban life, difficulties with linguistic adaptation, and the shock of cultural change—the sheer weight of numbers bore heavily upon urban schools. On the national scale, the balance of population was shifting inexorably from the rural to the urban, and the shift continued throughout the period. Of even greater significance, the number of truly urban concentrations exceeding 50,000 in population increased sharply from just 25 in 1870 to over 100 by 1910, and the proportion of school-age children in these centers had reached 25 percent by 1870 and continued to grow. Moreover, the trend involved not only older established cities in the previously urbanized regions of the Northeast and Old Northwest, but also cities of every age and type in nearly every section of the nation. Cities grew with astonishing rapidity, and the number of school children in their populations increased disproportionately. Greater numbers of students—in both absolute and relative terms—defied the physical capacities of city schools, and although some cities and regions felt the impact more severely, the phenomenon was nationwide. Even in centers highly urbanized by 1875, demographic changes occurred with sufficient rapidity to make adequate responses to novel conditions significantly more difficult.[2]

Although historical perspective brings demographic patterns into sharper focus, contemporary educators apparently recognized them quite clearly. In 1894 Commissioner of Education William Torrey Harris observed that the nation was becoming "less agricultural and more given to those diversified occupations for the pursuits of which the conditions represented by cities are the necessary concomitants." Even earlier, one of Harris's colleagues had remarked somewhat more directly and certainly more succinctly that "the simplicity of rural life is rapidly changing into a complex urban life with varied and urgent demands" upon city schools.[3]

Before any of those demands could be met, however, it was imperative that the city child be removed from the mill, factory, sweatshop, street—wherever socioeconomic conditions placed him—and relocated in the school where, educators sincerely believed, learning could alleviate the dislocations of the urban milieu. But despite determined efforts toward that end, particularly through a proliferation of compulsory attendance laws, in no city during the Gilded Age did enrollment rise significantly above 60 percent of the school-age population, and actual attendance remained substantially less. To be sure, observers found attendance rates slightly higher in urban areas than in the country, but even in the city, seasonal, occupational and economic factors, home conditions, resistance to compulsion in traditionally private matters, and public apathy negated legalistic efforts to raise attendance levels. Part of the failure involved the nature of compulsory attendance and child labor laws themselves and their frequent inconsistencies. Attendance legislation required only a minimal annual period in school prior to eligibility for employment. Connecticut alone required attendance for the full school term, and California's law demanding attendance for two-thirds of the regular term stood among the most stringent. Requirements elsewhere ranged from thirty weeks in Massachusetts to twelve weeks in sixteen states and territories, and definition of "school age" varied just as widely, from seven to sixteen years in Wyoming to ten to fourteen in Utah. Minimum ages for employment were similarly rendered meaningless by their ties to attendance legislation. Compliance with school attendance requirements could come at any time during the school year, and investigators found that children were always "just going to school" when parents or employers were questioned. Finally, few laws provided for enforcement, delegating that authority to teachers, truant officers, or the local constabulary, a flaw educators identified as critical.[4]

However, a multitude of vaguely defined exemptions further emasculated attendance laws. Poverty, distance, lack of clothing, sick parents, or simply "inability to send" or "urgent reasons" constituted acceptable extenuation. Furthermore, heavy penalties ranging up to $50 and a jail sentence—imposed on the parent or child rather than employers—tended to prevent enforcement. Penalties would have fallen mainly upon the poorer urban working classes, those of necessity most often in violation and least able to pay fines or serve sentences. Thus, a tangle of legalisms and urban socioeconomic conditions subverted the goals of attendance laws and made them particularly ineffective for the children of the poor for whose benefit they were initially intended. Indeed, conflicting legislation could, in effect, force children out of school and into the streets. In Illinois, for example, sixteen weeks of school fulfilled attendance requirements for children between ages seven and fourteen, and state law forbade employment under fourteen. Under such conditions, the child under fourteen who had met the annual attendance requirement could be neither legally employed nor compelled to attend school.[5]

Inadequate legislative coordination could obviously accomplish little to alleviate urban absenteeism. But even more importantly, despite energetic efforts, educators themselves failed to evaluate the extent of nonattendance or its causes accurately. One study, for example, involving twelve years' attendance data for three major cities, concluded that the average child remained in school until after his fifteenth birthday in Chicago and Boston and until his thirteenth birthday in St. Louis, despite findings of the Census Bureau and reformers like Jacob Riis to the contrary. Educators, however, relied upon school records which recorded only when children *left* school, whereas the census and reformers relied upon observation and included those who had *never* attended and appeared in no school data.[6]

Complacency may have resulted from educators' attendance studies which asked the wrong question, but their preconceptions concerning those who did not enroll in school conditioned attitudes even more effectively. Articulate spokesmen for the profession insisted that "children are with [the working classes] means of making money. A day at school is so much time lost." In 1882 Commissioner John Eaton echoed the sentiment: "Wherever the lawless classes or those who are driven by necessity or avarice to profit by the labor of their children are in great numbers, it becomes difficult to secure a high average of attendance." The great numbers were, of course, in cities. But Eaton, as did the majority of his contemporaries in the profession, ascribed greater significance to avarice among the urban working classes than to necessity, which constituted the reality of their lives. Among the thousands of urban families composing the group of which Eaton spoke, the paltry earnings of children were essential to the family's maintenance of even marginal status. This fact professional educators failed to consider in their evaluation of the attendance problem. Nor did they understand the price many of these families paid for maintenance of even marginal status: the future mobility of the children, locked into the condition of their parents by the lack of even rudimentary education.[7]

Little evidence indicates that Gilded Age urban educators evolved any positive understanding of socioeconomic condi-

tions in the city or seriously considered their impact upon
school attendance. They continued to assume that city children "of the least intelligent parents . . . are the last to seek
admission to the schools" and to give scant attention to the
realities which gave validity to the observation. They most
frequently presumed that factory children worked as a result
of the "heartless greed and often laziness" of parents, not
necessity. Even occasional pleas for an understanding of the
disabilities which precluded regular school attendance by
working class children were obviated by assumptions of parental
greed or misanthropy.[8] Most middle-class educators, particularly those at the policy-making levels of the professional
hierarchy, remained the captives of their preconceptions concerning the urban masses. Moreover, they remained essentially
isolated from those masses, a condition that precluded realistic
revision of entrenched assumptions.

Increasingly fragmented urban residential patterns well
may have impeded contact between educational leaders and
the working masses. However, nothing precluded a close
observation and analysis of practices and conditions in city
schools themselves, thereby adding to an understanding of
the attendance problem. Indeed, in the 1890s several concerned laymen did precisely that. Among them, Dr. Joseph M.
Rice toured the schools of several cities, and his critical
published reports reveal the "chaos" he found. Had urban
educators accompanied Rice and other lay critics, they might
have learned about absenteeism from the students' perspective. In St. Louis, for example, schools emphasized rigid
discipline while demanding rote answers, rather than intellectual activity. In a New York City school a principal's
concept of education, by his own admission, derived from
the maxim "Save the minutes," and rote memorization and
recitation were the teaching methods employed to implement
it. Coordinating even the physical movements of recitation
with the precision of a martial drill saved still more minutes.
In city after city, similar conditions prevailed: uninspired
teaching, irrelevant curricula, impossible physical facilities,

and methods which Rice categorized as "purely mechanical drudgery."[9] Such schools could have held little appeal for urban children and stimulated even less motivation to attend. Two decades later, educators might have learned still more about the realities of urban education from the child's perspective if they had accompanied an Illinois factory inspector through the manufacturing districts of Chicago. Children between eight and fourteen who appeared twice their age, dressed in ill-fitting cast-off clothing, working and coughing in the dust of mills or the heat and odors of tobacco and lacquer shops, explained their own attitudes toward school. Of 500 working children interviewed, 412 preferred the factory, even if their earnings were not essential to their families. One pale and dull-faced urchin asserted, "They ain't always picking on you because you don't know things in a factory," and another commented, "The boss never hits yer, er slaps yer face, er pulls yer ears, er makes you stay in at recess." Still another fatigued worker avowed bluntly, "What ye learn in school ain't no good. Ye get paid just as much in the factory if ye never was [in school]. Our boss he never went to school," and an eight-year-old girl looked up from her task in a cannery to state, "School ain't no good. The Holy Father can send you to hell, the boss he can take away yer job er raise yer pay. The teacher can't do nothing." And they were not called "Dago" or "Christ-killer" in the factories. Working also had more meaning for children than school. The oversized Polish or Lithuanian boy (or farm boy from Iowa), sitting at a desk too small for him in a room crowded with obviously younger children, subjected to their abuse and the teacher's obvious contempt for his ability to learn, could hardly find school as attractive as the factory, which at least paid him minimal wages,[10] particularly when what he was taught bore little relevance to his life. With greater sensitivity to such conditions, urban educators might have achieved greater success in their efforts to improve attendance.

But the Gilded Age produced neither altered attitudes nor significantly increased proportions of children in school. Nor did a growing trend toward required full-term attendance or occasional efforts to modify curricula. Indeed, as late as the 1905 NEA Convention Jane Addams continued to castigate educators for their failure to keep urban children in school and because they had apparently "lost all interest and responsibility and . . . turned the children over to the business world." Clearly, the persistent—though frequently misdirected—legalistic efforts of educators had failed to resolve the dual problem of nonattendance and child labor. Despite belated recognition that neither could be separated from the question of poverty among large portions of the urban population, despite reformers' concern for the content of the urban school curriculum, and despite increasing percentages of the population placed under compulsory education laws, the problems plagued educators well into the twentieth century.[11]

Ironically, effective legislation would have, in fact, aggravated another major problem of urban education in the Gilded Age. In 1890, Jacob Riis commented wryly on the futility of New York City truant officers' efforts to force children into classrooms as illogical "since the department that employs [them] admits that thousands of poor children are crowded out of the schools year by year for want of room." Space had always been a problem in urban schools, but by 1882 studies revealed insufficient accommodations for 55 percent of the nation's city children, and official reports from individual cities disclosed critical shortages. In 1881 New York City denied admission to 9,189 students because of inadequate space; in 1882 Philadelphia turned away a staggering 60,000 for similar reasons. Moreover, crowding characterized even existing facilities. In 1883, for example, common school classes in San Francisco averaged sixty students, the result of efforts to house a burgeoning student population. A decade later, Brooklyn Superintendent William H. Maxwell reported that in his city 477 classes contained over 60 students, 51 exceeded 100 students, and 4 had surpassed the almost inconceivable figure of 140 students under the direction of a single teacher.[12]

To cope with these incredible situations, many cities resorted to such expedients as the use of decrepit rental or portable buildings. Throughout the period, Chicago's rentals provided momentary but inadequate relief, while St. Louis, Milwaukee, and Boston employed equally unsatisfactory portables. But whether permanent or temporary, rented or owned, urban public schools in the Gilded Age were often less than attractive and frequently less than safe. As early as 1877, concerned educators surveyed urban schools and found poor heating and ventilation and odors from latrines and privies endemic in Boston schools; critical absence of ventilation and lack of space in Madison; odor, crowding, and poor ventilation in New Orleans; darkness severe enough to damage sight in Baltimore; foul air in Cincinnati; and all of these and worse in the schools of New York City. The perpetuation of similar circumstances over the following decades prompted one educator to complain that "Our city school-houses are at once our glory and our shame," and another to comment bluntly, "Too many [urban] school-houses are unfit to be used."[13]

Educators did not ignore such complaints, however. Indeed, the professional literature of the era is filled with discussions ranging from buildings, lighting, ventilation, and sanitation to the psychological effect of environment on learning; from vaccination codes in various cities to mental fatigue as a consequence of heredity; and from the intellectual and physiological influence of school seats upon children to the possibility of disease transmission through secondhand textbooks. Yet rarely was discussion translated into effective action. The same literature, as well as the observations of lay reporters, reveals little change before the turn of the century. In 1892 Chicago and Philadelphia still employed unsanitary and offensive partitions to turn assembly halls into classroom space, and Rice reported that Cincinnati school buildings remained "dark and gloomy, and [that] in many of them the laws of health are otherwise ignored, the classrooms being over-crowded and poorly ventilated," so packed that movement was restricted. Rice also found the physical condition of New York City schools deplorable, and another observer noted the self-congratulatory tone of the Brooklyn superintendent on actually having removed two cellars from service as classrooms. Still another reporter found one New York school where 768 children attended class "over the offensive live-chicken market in Essex street" and "dark, unfurnished rooms in Allen street where pupils study on their knees." Throughout the city, sausage factories, tenements, stables, and worse pressed in upon schools. Fumes from sanitary facilities wafted through windows, filth overran basement playrooms, janitors looted the little equipment available, and wooden or nonexistent fire escapes compounded hazards.[14]

To be sure, such reports produced responses; the New York City Public Education Association, for example, promoted the construction of 69 new school buildings at a cost to the city of over $12 million between 1895 and 1902. Nevertheless, the magnitude of the problem precluded complete solution, and New York City school children, particularly the poor, continued to study under grossly detrimental circumstances. Moreover, New York's experience was only the extreme; throughout the nation, differences were only those of degree. Indeed, only rarely were school facilities, usually those of a relatively new city like Denver, found worthy of praise.[15]

In tead, assessments at the turn of the century varied little from those of the previous two decades. In five entire wards, Philadelphia children still attended overcrowded schools, sat on floors or used soap boxes for chairs and desks, or found themselves in a kindergarten "located between the water closets used by 900 pupils, so that the only outside air comes from these places with no [other] ventilation of any kind." In the nation's capital, where children overcrowded even two-year-old structures, 40 of 83 school buildings were adjudged seriously in excess of capacity.

Buffalo utilized "annexes" never intended for school use —as did Boston and Washington—and pressed into service attics, hallways, basements, cloakrooms, and even principals' offices. In Boston, despite similar expedients, many children could not enter school at all and thousands of others "crowded into inadequate spaces, often ill-ventilated, and unsanitary buildings that are crumbling with age." In San Francisco a similar situation prevailed; there it proved difficult to discover a "single, modern, properly equipped grade [school] building," and many schools were so old, run-down, and unsanitary that they constituted hazards to health and safety.[16] In view of the volume and persistence of such contemporary evaluations, the conclusion that deficient school facilities represented a national problem in the late 1800s is difficult to avoid.

However, factors other than antiquated buildings, poor maintenance, crowding, and unsanitary conditions impeded effective education. Many cities resorted to shortened sessions, thereby compounding the problem. In 1893, for example, 16,000 Minneapolis children in the first three grades attended school for only half a day, and Philadelphia had 8,000 in similar circumstances. The District of Columbia resorted to abbreviated sessions in most schools in black districts of the city. Other cities employed more teachers than available classrooms to achieve similar ends. Teachers, after all, cost less than buildings, but the practice could hardly be other than detrimental to education. The Baltimore school which in 1893 contained 950 students, 21 teachers, and only 12 rooms perhaps represented the extreme. Nevertheless, cities across the nation resorted to shortened sessions or simultaneous use of classroom space or both in efforts to solve their problems. And both measures bore especially heavily upon the children of the urban poor. For in the densely populated "lower wards" where they were most frequently employed, the prevalent necessity of leaving school to work already circumscribed educational opportunity.[17]

Yet the poor were not alone in their exposure to the inadequacies which were general in all but a few cities. Rice, for example, found "some of the most unhealthful schools in [New York City] being attended by children from the best homes," and there is little to indicate that his assessment would be less appropriate for other cities.[18]

The precise reasons that a nation intensely committed to the ideal of education for all should have failed for a generation to send many of its urban children to school, or to provide for them adequately once there, are somewhat elusive. To be sure, economic factors, including cyclic depressions throughout the period and a tendency toward municipal retrenchment under the shibboleth of "reform," retarded progress significantly. So, too, did general resistance to taxation. Moreover, the public, school boards, and city governments, though still devoted in principle to education, were distracted by urbanization, unable to anticipate future needs, and unwilling to provide schools for more than immediate needs. And the persistent involvement of ward, city, and state politics— particularly partisan maneuverings for patronage—also hindered progress. Nor should the inexperience of municipal leadership be discounted. Faced with unprecedented growth, the seemingly unlimited opportunity of burgeoning industrialism, and wildly climbing urban land values, decision makers frequently diverted their resources toward ventures more lucrative than school construction. As a consequence, the demands of urban education often went unheeded, despite swelling school budgets and expenditures.[19]

However, the shortcomings of educational responses to urbanization in the Gilded Age involved much more than economic considerations, and no attempt to understand the failures may ignore either the urbanization process itself or its subtle implications. For example, both contemporary observers and recent historians of the city have shown the fragmentation of the surburban process well under way prior to the turn of the century. M. A. DeWolfe Howe had already commented that "the conditions of city life have never before emphasized the division [between economic and social classes] as it is emphasized today," and settlement worker Robert Archey Woods, using Boston as an example, described the results of growing separation between classes. For both Howe and Woods, the city had become a "wilderness" characterized by animal-like individualism and lack of sympathy and understanding among most of its residents. Not even cities less directly influenced by industrialization and immigration escaped the process of fragmentation. By the 1880s transportation technology and the desire of better citizens to escape the urban center had transformed cities like Wilmington, Delaware, into three distinct sections with little contact among them: the suburbs, the area of the "plain people," and the slums.[20]

This same process of urban fragmentation explains, at least partially, why members of the decision-making classes—including educational leaders—did not clearly understand the realities of urban conditions. It may also explain why, unlike Rice, Riis, and other socially oriented reformers, educators failed to recognize the true conditions of the city schools or the urgency of their problems. Growing separation, coupled with traditional patterns of thought and often with antiurban sentiments, led many educators to consider child labor an inevitable adjunct of urban-industrial society, to assume that the greed of parents and not socioeconomic conditions explained nonattendance, to resort to crowding rather than school construction, and to articulate unwarranted confidence in the state of education in the nation's cities. For despite the genuine concern and effort of Gilded Age educators, and despite the responsibility that school boards, politicians, and an apathetic public share, it must be concluded that educators failed to solve the problems of attendance and facilities, which John Eaton had identified for them a generation earlier. Indeed, many continued to share with Eaton the complacent belief that the nation's best school work was being done in city classrooms.[21]

2

The Urban Impact:

Professionalism

> *Education is much more than a great and noble art; it is a noble science.*
> —Burke A. Hinsdale

By the last quarter of the nineteenth century, urbanization had concentrated unprecedented numbers of teachers in cities, drawing them by the same forces and conditions that created problems of attendance, crowding, and inadequate facilities in the schools themselves. Though numbers were neither sufficient for the task in the Gilded Age nor spectacular by current standards, in a period prior to the emergence of the metropolitan school district, they were noteworthy indeed. For example, in 1875, twenty years before creation of the "Greater New York City" public school system, the city employed more than 3,000 teachers; that same year three other cities employed over 1,000, three others over 700, and two more than 500.[1]

Such major concentrations, contrasting sharply with scatterings of teachers in the countryside, should have given impetus to professional organization and the interchange of ideas and ultimately to significant improvement in both the status and competence of urban teachers. Urbanization did facilitate such trends, but impetus should not be confused with accomplishment. Despite the formation of dozens of teachers' organizations in urban centers and the opportunity they presented, real achievement in the growth of professionalism remained minimal, particularly if academic training is used as a criterion. As late as 1931 only 10 percent of all elementary teachers had earned the bachelor's degree, and not until 1952 did a majority attain that standard. It should not be assumed, however, that Gilded Age urban teachers made no effort to elevate their profession; they were among the first to move in that direction. And at least a tentative relationship exists between the pattern of urbanization and the establishment of local teachers' organizations dedicated to increased professionalism. To be sure, associations did exist prior to the late 1800s, but their number increased sharply as urban concentration accelerated. Teachers founded only 5 local groups in the 1870s but established 37 in the first decade of the twentieth century, and the rate of their creation closely paralleled the process of urbanization.[2]

As local associations emerged, they worked for both social and professional improvement of their members by promoting concerts, excursions, and other entertainments, sponsoring lectures on moral and pedagogical topics, and disseminating information on educational innovations, including the ideas of kindergartener Friedrich Froebel and child psychologist Johann Herbart as well as developments emanating from the NEA. For a time few organizations offered accredited academic work for the advancement of their members and occasionally influenced the policy of school administration.[3]

However, the critical policy-making role of local teacher organizations became a casualty of urbanization. Prior to the centralization of city school administration, local groups did have significant influence because the laymen in control of educational programs frequently sought teachers' advice. But the late nineteenth-century advent of the professional superintendent and the accompanying bureaucracy effectively negated the policy-making role of teacher groups which thereafter concentrated upon more mundane concerns. The New York Teachers' Association, for example, established a life insurance program in 1869, and Brooklyn followed in 1871, Jersey City in 1880, and Camden (N.J.) in 1885. Ironically, in this aspect of their activities local groups did influence school systems successfully; in 1894, New York City teachers induced the city to initiate the first publicly supported pension program, a practice adopted by more than seventy cities by 1900.

But such was the limit of the organizations' influence on policy. Retirement programs had undeniable importance in an era of low teacher earnings, but city teachers also lost an equally important function of their professional life—their role in planning and directing curriculum, choosing textbooks, and guiding educational policy—at least partially in consequence of urban tendencies toward centralization. In response, Margaret Haley, president of the National Federation of Teachers in 1904, called for organization at local, state, and national levels to recoup those losses, to counter business and political influences in education, to participate in the fight against municipal corruption, and to reassert professional influence in the conduct of schools.[4] There is little evidence, however, of great urban classroom teacher response to her appeal.

Nor did teachers achieve notably greater success in their efforts toward academic self-improvement. Despite persistent discussions of new methods and concepts of education, urban teachers at the turn of the century remained more remarkable for mediocrity or even incompetence than for proficiency or professionalism. However, only a minor portion of the responsibility may be attributed to the success or failure of local organizations. Indeed, those voluntary associations raised the standards of those they reached, and their very existence evidences an awareness among urban teachers themselves of the pressing need for higher degrees of academic and professional proficiency. Furthermore, the massiveness of the problem and the transitory nature of the profession virtually precluded major achievement through organizing teachers and demanded more universal action by cities themselves as well as by states. Rural and urban educators alike recognized that demand throughout the Gilded Age. One administrator, looking back over a twenty-year career, evaluated the consequences of defective teacher preparation with unusual candor: "I shudder to think of the innocent victims sacrificed to make me the moderately successful pedagogue that I am."[5]

There can be little doubt that urban concentration made such sacrifices more numerous and educators more aware of them. Burgeoning city school populations created a constant demand which could be met only by pressing into service, albeit reluctantly, applicants with minimal qualifications and hoping to train them after they had begun to teach. Toward that end, numerous cities resorted to the expedient of the in-service teacher institute. Of origins more rural than urban, the institute emanated from the Chattaqua movement which it resembled in more ways than one but became a major feature of city teacher-training programs as early as the 1870s. Although institutes retained much of their rural flavor and often something of their camp-meeting fervor, they also acquired distinctive features in the urban setting. Five-to-ten-day affairs held in the weeks preceding the opening of the fall school term, city institutes lost their voluntary character and became compulsory for urban teachers. Indeed, the relative ease of urban transportation often made institutes semiannual events in the city, and before the end of the century several states had made institutes mandatory in both urban and rural school districts and even provided financial support. Nevertheless, despite educators' nearly universal faith in the institute as a means of upgrading teaching—a faith that remains only slightly diminished today—and the growing diversification, specialization, and sophistication which urban concentration encouraged, the institute remained superficial at best, a generally ineffective substitute for formal academic training. In fact, the "annual swelter of an August institute" frequently acted as a detriment to teaching morale and perhaps even as an impediment to ambitions to acquire more extensive professional training. Still, the annual or semiannual institute became a permanent feature of the city school system, and in one year 251,768 teachers attended 2,579 institutes totaling 21,748 day.[6]

But even such massive efforts at training teachers could neither meet the needs of growing cities nor raise the general level of teacher competence sufficiently, and rapid urban growth forced administrators and school boards to seek alternate means toward those ends. The adaptation of another non-urban institution, the normal school, which had been a state or private academy designed to supply teachers to rural and county schools, provided the alternative. Even before the end of the Civil War, New York City, Philadelphia, San Francisco, Baltimore, Newark, Brooklyn, St. Louis, Trenton, and numerous other cities had established normal schools to provide teachers for their exploding school populations, and by 1874 nine cities had expanded their programs to two years. Slightly more than a decade later, the number had increased to 22, and by the first decade of the twentieth century, every city but one with a population over 300,000 and 80 percent of those over 100,000 operated municipal normal schools.[7]

Although city normal schools proliferated in the Gilded Age and educators placed great faith in them, they neither supplied the necessary quantity of teachers nor prepared even those who attended either academically or pedagogically. In 1899, public normal schools enrolled just 56,279 students and graduated only 11,175, scarcely one-fourth of the new teachers needed in that year alone. Moreover, neither the background of the students admitted nor the content of the normal schools' curricula promised great professional growth. Although urban institutions frequently set higher standards of admission than others and occasionally even required high school graduation for enrollment, most who entered were only grammar school graduates and often not even that. As late as 1908 the NEA Department of Normal Schools felt constrained to offer a resolution recommending high school as a prerequisite for normal school, a standard not universal until 1930.[8] Entrants' prior education understandably inhibited the level of work offered in normal schools, for it necessitated "proficiency" courses in subjects taught in grammar school and thereby detracted from work in both advanced academic areas and educational theory and practice.

Curricula in city normal schools varied widely, dependent

upon local conditions and standards. Most offered a two-year
course of study, which included both academic and pedagogical
work, approximately equivalent to the first two years of high
school. Cities that, like New York, could require high school
graduation for admission offered more extensive training in
both areas and included supervised practice teaching in their
programs. The majority, however, until they were absorbed by
state college systems or other institutions, provided little more
than a rudimentary education and professional training for
their students. Less than one-fourth of those who entered
normal schools ever completed the course before entering the
classroom as teachers. Thus, the normal school, like the
teachers' institute, led to little significant improvement in the
quality of education available in Gilded Age urban schools.
For example, in Massachusetts, which had the best trained
teachers in the nation in 1890, less than 40 percent of all
teachers had attended a normal school, only one-third had
graduated from such an institution, and the vast majority had
a high school education or less.[9]

Yet normal schools in general and urban normal schools
in particular did contribute to the acceptance of teaching as a
profession by laying the groundwork for future developments.
To be sure, many academics, like the crusty President Charles
W. Eliot of Harvard, felt "but slight interest or confidence in
what is commonly called pedagogy," but many more had both
interest and confidence. By the turn of the century, although
few city superintendents had confidence that normal school
graduates could prove effective high school teachers, 80 percent admitted that they sought college graduates, with or without work in education, indicating a clear recognition of the
value of advanced training. And although teachers themselves
began to question the value of normal schools, increasing numbers, without coercion enrolled in other institutions in order to
advance themselves personally and professionally. The trend
toward higher learning for teachers seemed to hold great hope
for professionalism and inspired one pedagogue to assert con-
fidently that "education is much more than a great art; it is a

noble science" to be taught as a major discipline in colleges and universities. Simultaneously, more cautious minds like that of Nicholas Murray Butler evaluated the "pedagogics now being taught at colleges and universities" as the "merest nonsense." Nevertheless, he too was convinced of the imminent emergence of a teaching profession.[10]

However, major accomplishments in urban education were limited. Indeed, the creation of city normal schools may even have retarded progress by stimulating provincialism and furthering stagnation, particularly when "outsiders" were rejected in order to provide positions for local normal school products. Moreover, the absence of consistent and known standards for certification and the granting of credentials by local authorities tended to further undermine whatever progress normal schools and other institutions made and permitted political patronage to infest urban educational systems. In 1898 only three state governments controlled the issuance of teaching certificates; all the others left the matter principally to local agencies. These same conditions—indefinite standards, local control, and political involvement—also undermined the one quantitative measure of professionalism, monetary reward. Although slightly more liberal than rural districts in terms of both salaries and other school expenditures, cities paid teachers approximately the wages commanded by semiskilled artisans, hardly an index of professional status.[11] (See Tables 2.1 and 2.2.)

Singularly improved performance in the classroom itself would furnish less tangible but more convincing evidence of professionalism. However, despite interminable metaphysical debates conducted in the pages of educational journals, reports and other publications of the NEA and U.S. Bureau of Education, and on the floor of NEA conventions and other meetings, rarely were discussions translated into action in city classrooms. In the upper echelons of the profession, pedagogical controversy raged, a jargon developed, and the thought of Pestalozzi, Froebel, and Herbart underwent dissection and clinical examination. Methodological and psychological innovations—includ-

ing object teaching, concentration of studies, and child study—
were subjected to similar treatment. Yet their principles rarely
penetrated to the practice of city school teachers.

Table 1
Rural and Urban Teachers's Weekly Salary, 1875–1905[a]

	Rural[b]		Urban	
	Men	Women	Men	Women
1875	$11.46	$ 8.00	$36.63	$12.69
1880	9.73	7.46	31.36	12.20
1885	10.95	8.23	33.15	13.24
1890	11.30	8.55	36.62	13.16
1895	11.70	8.91	31.63	13.40
1900	12.13	8.93	31.54	13.88
1905	14.39	10.15	33.79	14.86

a. From Warren R. Burgess, *Trends of School Costs* (New York: Russell Sage Foundation, 1920), pp. 32-33.

b. The rural school term was usually less than half the urban, averaging 10 to 15 weeks as opposed to 20 to 30.

Table 2
Teachers' Annual Salary in Selected Cities, 1905*

Allegheny, Pa.	$500– 900	Portland, Ore.	$550– 850
Boston	552–1212	Providence, R.I.	500– 900
Chicago	550–1225	Pueblo, Col.	550– 750
Cleveland	500– 900	Sacramento	700–1000
Denver	635–1010	San Francisco	720– 840
Kansas City, Mo.	500– 825	Seattle	540– 864
Lowell, Mass.	500– 600	Tacoma	500– 750
Newark, N.J.	520–1000	Washington, D.C.	600–1350
New York City	600–2400		

*From *USAR (1904/05)*, I, 224-228.

Although educators and administrators paid lip service to
new concepts and, apparently convinced by their own rhetoric,
indulged in sanctimonious self-adulation concerning the progress of the profession, reality belied the confidence of most.
Indeed, Andrew S. Draper, New York State Commissioner of
Education and himself formerly a superintendent of several
city school systems, felt compelled to observe in 1899:

With exceptions so rare that they do not count, the teachers in
the elementary schools of all the greater American cities are
tramping around in small circles which are very nearly on the
same plane; and the schools do little more than mark time in
endless routine.

Furthermore, even teachers who had acquired a modicum of professional training and comprised the "exceptions so rare" hesitated to apply their knowledge, intimidated by school officials less knowledgeable than they and by the rigidity of the systems in which they labored. Such conditions, argued Charles W. Eliot, degraded "the teacher's function, and converts his occupation, which should be varied and inspiring, into a killing routine which runs its round in a single year."[12]

Admittedly, Gilded Age city teachers labored under conditions that virtually prohibited either their students' progress or their own satisfaction. And they could expect but little guidance from the few—and often politically appointed—supervisors employed to train and assist them. Moreover, attempts to change curricular content remained in the realm of heady discussions rather than concrete proposals, and in 1892 William H. Maxwell, Superintendent of Schools in Brooklyn (and later New York City), observed that despite efforts to expand and diversify, common school curricula lagged 25 years behind and remained "for the most part in the hands of the Philistines." Suggestions that programs be brought "more in line with the immediate demands of actual life" faced the two-fold impediment of inertia—tenacious commitment to traditional courses and methods and to the values of the rural-agrarian past. To be sure, theorists insisted that reading be taught as a tool skill, that mathematics be related to life situations, that grammar be subordinated to the "practical art of using language," that details be eliminated from history and geography in favor of concepts and principles, and that natural history and civics become important parts of the curriculum. However, little concrete change occurred either in curricular content, methods employed, or consideration for the needs of the individual student. Unfortunately, one contemporary's assessment, "our school was modern—hence the laboratory and the one hour a week for drawing," remained all too applicable to conditions in most cities.[13]

But the practice of teachers in the classroom remained even less beneficial or progressive. Despite criticisms of the

American teacher's tendency to flirt with vague pedagogical innovations, the affair was quite innocent and never consumated, and rigid discipline, rote learning, and reliance upon textbook recitation persisted as the major interests in classrooms. The fault, however, was not entirely with teachers, who also complained that "the public schools were excessively and injuriously mechanical" and that even the competent teacher found himself reduced to the status of a "mere automaton" by oversized classes, inadequate training, increasing rigidity of urban school systems, and incompetent superiors.[14]

For whatever reasons, substandard teaching persisted as a characteristic of urban schools throughout the Gilded Age. Rice's 1892 survey of education in common schools from Boston to St. Louis left little doubt of that fact. He found intellectual activity stifled, illogical methods reducing potentially beneficial innovations to the ridiculous, children's answers pronounced wrong for containing too much information, excessive emphasis on discipline, drill—frequently to the staccato rhythm of a cane on the desk—the favored teaching method, and teachers themselves generally insensitive.[15] Moreover, other observers, including professionals, tended to support Rice's muckraking study. Charles W. Eliot, for example, compared urban school methods to military drill, another found rigidity obviating learning, and still another assessed teachers as crude, rude, and sarcastic. And children supplied the most telling indictment: asked why they went to school, some replied, "to keep my pencil sharp" or "to sit in place." Obviously, the philosophical debates of pedagogical leaders had not penetrated their classrooms. And just as obviously, despite the opportunities the city afforded, urban teachers remained something less than progressive or professional.[16]

At the turn of the century, Rice asked why teachers lacked professional status and answered that they deserved little. It may have been an unfair assessment, but many agreed, including a principal who found "lack of confidence in teachers well grounded" since most of them considered their profession a mere way station on the way to something better. Men particularly regarded teaching as a makeshift and resisted specialized training for a temporary position which all but the least competent soon abandoned. Indeed, a 1908 survey of teachers reported that most men still regarded teaching only as a way out of the agricultural or industrial classes, and most women considered it a means of self-support while awaiting marriage. But even more detrimental to professionalism, "no one had ever thought through the problem of what education or teaching should be," except rhetorically. Therefore, nothing resembling a philosophy of education on which to build a profession emerged in the Gilded Age. The NEA grew, but it was top heavy with administrators and included less than 10 percent of the nation's half-million teachers by 1905,[17] and local organizations expanded only moderately and sporadically. Inadequate professional training, political involvements in education, constantly increasing demands for teachers in cities, and the attitudes of teachers and their superiors toward the profession all diluted whatever opportunities for professional development urbanization may have offered.

However, urbanization did bring significant modifications in two important aspects of the educational profession. One of these involved an accelerating tendency toward feminization. Beginning with the Civil War years, and perhaps more as a result of the manpower shortage that conflict created than of the urban process, increasing numbers of women became teachers. Yet this development closely paralleled urban growth. In 1870, women accounted for just half of all teachers, but by 1910 the proportion had expanded to nearly 80 percent. The growth of cities created unprecedented demands for teachers, and women who could be employed more cheaply than men, particularly in the city's graded classrooms, filled increasing numbers of positions in urban schools. Although contemporaries debated the merits of the transformation, it seems rather clear that the change ultimately benefited especially the younger children.[18]

Of greater immediate and long-range significance than the feminization of teaching was the second transformation related to urbanization. As a direct consequence of the growth of cities, the urban school administrator assumed a position of preeminence. Indeed, he alone attained a status even approaching professionalism; he became the dominant figure in and the major spokesman for American public education. School systems necessitated by the demands of mass education provided platforms from which dynamic superintendents might gain state and even national authority and recognition, and in many cases the NEA facilitated the process. Although the Department of Superintendence dates from 1865 and from 1875 as an adjunct of the national association, after 1875 urban administrators, their ideas, and their attitudes emerged as a controlling force within the NEA and thus throughout the profession. Of 90 nationally elected NEA officers (president, secretary, treasurer) chosen between 1875 and 1905, 61 positions were filled by men who were city superintendents, 5 by city principals, and 2 more by officers of the Department of Superintendence.[19]

Administrative dominance, however, provides only the most apparent evidence of the superintendents' growing influence and the acceptance of their leadership and ideologies. City administrators disseminated their ideas not only through speeches at annual meetings of the national organization, which they dominated,[20] but also through the pages of lay and professional journals to which they contributed prolifically. Moreover, concepts of organization and efficiency, the core of the thought of these nascent pedagogical bureaucrats, rapidly became the principal dogmas of urban educational reform movements in the Gilded Age and persisted in educational thought in subsequent generations.

Thus, the rise of the city school administrator had significant consequences. Such officials not only shared common ideas and transformed them into NEA policy, but also codified those ideas into what might be termed the first national conception of education in the United States. The fecundity of the administrators' literary output, supported by their growing status, drew attention to the unique problems of city schools.

But most important for the subsequent history of American education, the concepts city superintendents sought to apply to urban problems—organization, centralization, and bureaucratization—rapidly became accepted as educational principles in both urban and rural school systems across the nation.

3

Efficiency, Centralization, and Bureaucracy

> *Without question the greatest problem today is how best to administer the public school interests of a great city.*
>
> Aaron Gove

There can be little doubt that the characteristics of urbanization—concentration, diversification, and explosive populations—and their attendant problems provided the setting for increasing bureaucracy in public education, its growing rigidity, and the city administrator's rise to dominance in the educational profession. It is also evident that schoolmen recognized, somewhat regretfully, that altered conditions seriously challenged their preconceptions of the nature of both society and education and made unique demands upon the city schools. But only rarely did Gilded Age educators attack the problems of urbanization frontally. Instead, they marshaled their forces to assault the bastions of disorganization and inefficiency in management—a strategy which persisted throughout the period. Commissioner of Education John Eaton summarized the questions occupying urban educators early in the period when he wrote in 1877:

Some of the greatest excellences of American education are found in [city] systems, but we are reaching a point in their administration where various questions are arising which suggest a careful revision of the whole field of public school education in our great centres of population; . . . to the thoughtful student there comes the suggestion that there are among us cities enough

43

. . . to begin to point [to] methods of organization and administration

to assure both immediate and permanent improvement. The tone Eaton set for the solution of urban educational problems changed little before the turn of the century when Superintendent Aaron Gove of Denver continued to assert that "Without question the greatest problem today is how best to administer the public school interests of a great city," and virtually dismissed considerations of the nature and content of education.[1] Since the views of Eaton and Gove coincided closely with those of the vast majority of their colleagues, efforts to reform the Gilded Age city public school focused not on the classroom but on organization and resulted in a highly centralized bureaucratic system which most often precluded rather than facilitated genuine, durable reform.

The initial concept of city school systems organized under the aegis of a paid administrative official was not an invention of urban educators in the late 1800s, nor was education the main motivation. Early urban growth had made such a course seem desirable, if not inevitable. During the Jacksonian Era, school management usually termed "inspection," typically placed responsibility for both school administration and teacher guidance in the hands of boards of unpaid laymen. As cities grew, their responsibilities, frequently involving school visitation and teacher training, became burdensome and usurped time from the conduct of private affairs. Indeed, many school officials either resigned or refused reelection to their positions. In response, in 1837 Buffalo became the first city to employ a full-time superintendent; Louisville, St. Louis, Providence, Springfield, Rochester, and New Orleans followed suit within five years.[2] Thus originated an institution which would be universal in urban education by the end of the century.

Early city superintendents, however, were most often laymen chosen by local boards and rarely more qualified professionally than the inspectors or visitors they succeeded, Consequently, they were barred from any major administrative responsibility and were confined to visiting schools, supervising and evaluating teachers, and conducting training sessions. They did serve to free school board members who continued to possess the real authority from time-consuming tasks and allowed them to concentrate on substantive educational matters and private affairs. This early impetus toward paid urban school superintendency involved not the desire to improve or systematize education but the need to reduce responsibilities of lay school board members, and the innovation altered the organization and function of antebellum city school systems only slightly.[3] Yet it did establish a precedent to be built upon in the Gilded Age.

Another early urban innovation would provide a similar but more immediately significant precedent. The replacement of nongraded classrooms by rigidly graded schools began before the Civil War and continued unabated until the turn of the century when "the pendulum had swung from the extreme of no system to the extreme of all system." Superintendent John D. Philbrick of the Boston suburb of Quincy usually receives credit for the change; in 1847 he replaced traditional large halls and their appended recitation rooms with individual classrooms and teachers assigned to instruct specific age levels. This new system improved not only discipline and efficiency in schools but also the effectiveness of teachers, and so impressed educators generally that within 15 years 28 cities had adopted some form of the plan. By 1885 it had achieved acceptance in American cities everywhere except in the South.[4]

These two early nineteenth-century urban developments, the employment of superintending officers and the introduction of graded schools, set the stage for the emergence of the hierarchical systems of school organization and administration now familiar throughout the United States. It remained only to erect a sound and centralized edifice upon the foundation, and the ideologies of municipal reform in the Gilded Age—organization, efficiency, management, expertise, and nonpartisanship—as familiar to educators and reformers as to politicians and businessmen, supplied the impetus, methods, and programs.

In 1885 Philbrick summarized what would be basic school reform dogma for a generation:

The history of city systems of schools makes it evident that in the matter of administration the tendency is towards a greater centralization and permanency of authority and that this tendency is in the direction of progress and improvement. No doubt excessive decentralization of administration has been one of the chief obstacles to improvement in every department of our free school systems.

Twenty-five years later, Ellwood Cubberly still recognized "many signs of an increasing centralization of management which will ultimately lead to greater efficiency." Signs there were, indeed, as there had been throughout the interim separating the two educators' comments. For even before the advent of Frederick Winslow Taylor and the cult of efficiency, the rhetoric and practice of urban educators revealed commitment to the ideas and ideals that would characterize Taylor's program. Furthermore, educators in the Gilded Age anticipated the individual precepts of the Taylor model: personal efficiency characterized by disciplined labor, efficient use of energy and a favorable input-output ratio (with the school system substituted for the factory), economic efficiency involving a favorable return on investment, social efficiency equated with social harmony, and above all, scientific and professional management.[5]

"[A city school system] may be understood in two ways," wrote Burke A. Hinsdale, former Cleveland Superintendent, in 1898. "It may mean the organization of studies, books, teaching and discipline found in one of our cities, or the organization of political functions and agents that stand behind these educational powers and make them possible."[6] But like so many of his contemporary colleagues, Hinsdale sought solutions to urban school problems more often through reorganizing political functions (more properly structures) and agents than through reform and reinterpretation of the basic concept of education. To be sure, discussions of pedagogical techniques and developments in psychology continued undiminished. But major efforts to alter the school bore upon its concrete structure rather than upon its less tangible content or function and embodied the principles of management-oriented administrators. As such officials came to dominate their profession, their ideologies also became the guiding principles of urban school reform.

Those ideologies could be summarized in a single word: "system," which embodied the precepts of efficiency, centralization of authority and responsibility, and division of powers. And "system" occupied the preeminent position in the thought of educational reformers throughout the nation in the late 1800s. Although proposals for reorganization in specific cities varied according to local conditions, all involved common principles—namely, nonpartisan school boards small enough to be efficient and responsible, expert superintendents and assistants to administer the system, fiscal authority divorced from other municipal agencies, extensive data and record keeping, and definitive separation between the legislative duties of school boards and the executive responsiblity of the superintendent and his staff. In short, educators sought and strove toward hierarchically organized, structured bureaucratic systems which would have basis in law and be amenable to sound management and attractive to good men. So pervasive was the appeal of efficiency and system, and so rapid their implementation, that by 1885, cities that still retained the "antiquated district system so long disapproved by every intelligent school man" were disdained for their provincialism.[7]

Twenty years later, Superintendent Gove of Denver could assert with little fear of contradiction that education "is comparable to the work of an industrial establishment, the performance of a task assigned by a police chief of a city, or communicated to a soldier while on duty," and that the role of a city superintendent was necessarily an autocratic one comparable to that of the secretary of war. Not a few educators compared the school to the factory; nor was Gove alone in employing the military metaphor. Superintendent William H. Maxwell of New York City utilized it a year later, even though he conceived of educational efficiency in a broader context including the ideas of social harmony and economic productivity. Nevertheless, management by powerful professional experts remained a central tenet of his and other educators' concept of efficient education in the late nineteenth-century city. Indeed, many considered the dearth of such university-trained officials as the single most serious detriment to sound city schools, and feared the involvement of laymen in education not only as an encroachment into the expert's domain but also as wasteful and grossly inefficient.[8]

From a generation of concentration upon system and expertise in education, there emerged by the turn of the century a set of values which were national in scope, anticipating and reflecting aspects of the efficiency movement in industry and progressivism in politics, and creating educational establishments dedicated to organization, often for its own sake. The resultant systems ossified and became inflexible and fraught with all the inbred rigidity of full-blown bureaucracies. Although a degree of variety did exist in the particulars of concepts advocated by individual educators, and the applications of their ideas differed among cities, a general consensus concerning the ideology, structure, and operation of "good" urban schools is apparent. Indeed, it is possible, from what the educational bureaucrats of the Gilded Age said and wrote, to construct a model of the system that would have existed if the major features of that consensus were implemented in the educational system of a single city.

Although reformers never achieved that goal, it would have been considered the epitome of educational efficiency. At the foundation of the ideal system would be a firm anchor in law, either in one of the municipal charters which proliferated in the reform frenzy of the Gilded Age or in a substantial body of local and state legislation, establishing the essential forms of the scheme and fixing the relationships among its components. A popularly elected school board, small enough to be efficient and with long terms staggered to ensure continuity, would provide the essential democratic veneer. Board members would be chosen, however, not to represent wards as before, but from the city at large and preferably at special elections, thus eliminating partisanship—anathema to educational and municipal reformers alike—and effectively limiting choices to business and professional men and community leaders rather than party hacks.

Duties prescribed for trustees no longer would include personnel matters, except ratification of administrative actions. Instead, board authority and responsibility would be restricted to legislative functions involving site acquisition, expenditures for building and maintenance, awarding contracts, and approving the policy, personnel, and instructional recommendations of the city's chief educational executive, the superintendent. Ideally, the board would select for that post a university-trained expert in education, chosen on the basis of civil service principles—training, qualification, and examination—and appoint him to a term sufficiently long for his personal service to bear fruit. The superintendent would dominate the city school system through nearly absolute control over, and responsibility for, the actual organization and operation of schools. As an *ex officio* member of the school board and its principal adviser, the superintendent also would be instrumental in both initiating and approving urban school policy. It is difficult to ignore the similarity between the superintendent and his staff and a corporate board of directors in charge of a highly structured and efficient industrial enterprise, precisely the sort of body educators sought to emulate.

Each assistant would have his own subordinates including supervisors, special teachers, custodial and maintenance personnel, principals and vice-principals of rigidly graded schools in lower hierarchical echelons, and finally the teaching staff and students. At each level, control and authority would flow from above, and responsibility, records, progress reports on individuals and the system itself would flow upward to be either analyzed, acted upon, or stored. Those in the lower ranks would move, through civil service examinations and evaluations of performance, to ever higher levels in the hierarchy: teachers to administrative posts, principals to supervisory positions, and supervisors into the city administration itself. Everywhere above the classroom level, all would be orderly, organized, and efficient, making the long-sought bureaucracy an apparent reality.[9]

Certainly, no single urban school system had all of the features of the model. Nor did educational bureaucracies spring Minerva-like into being in a single moment. Yet in the final quarter of the century, the principles and structures of the bureaucracy became a nationally accepted mode for combating educational problems in cities large and small, as the city-manager and commission systems with which they had much in common would become the accepted methods of the city government in the early twentieth century. New York City, for example, had at mid-century a moderately centralized system which it strengthened in 1873 by ending ward representation on the city school board. In 1896 it completed even the physical centralization of the system by absorbing surrounding districts into the "Greater City" system under the administration of a single superintendent. Boston, too, began a tendency toward centralization and bureaucracy early in the century; by 1876 Bostonians had reduced the size of the school committee from 97 to 24 and shifted control from lay board members to expert professional administrators. Somewhat inconsistently, however, Boston left its school board with veto power over the superintendent, causing dissension until remedied in 1904.[10]

In contrast, Baltimore's school system remained decentralized until a new city charter in 1898 abolished selection of school board members by ward while permitting the board to retain control over all educational matters, despite the appointment of the nationally renowned superintendent, James H. Van Sickle. Baltimore's hybrid system was the exception, however, for across the nation in the 1880s and 1890s cities either organized centralized bureaucratic school systems or reinforced those already existing. In 1892 both Cincinnati and Cleveland adopted such plans, featuring small citywide school boards and powerful superintendencies; Milwaukee emulated their action five years later, and Chicago, after appointing a committee to study the matter in 1897, received a similar plan in 1903.[11]

Farther west in St. Louis, centralization came during the administration of Superintendent William Torrey Harris (1868–1880), and new school laws in 1897 firmly established the bureaucratic pattern by increasing the authority of the superintendent and reducing the size and responsibility of the school board. Denver had created a centralized system in 1877, and it became even more bureaucratic under the leadership of its dynamic superintendent Aaron Gove in subsequent decades. Cities on the Pacific coast followed similar patterns. But San Francisco remained unique in that its charter of 1898 provided for a commission-type, paid, bipartisan school board and a popularly elected superintendent. Even smaller cities submitted to the bureaucratic urge, Portland, Oregon, originated a centralized school system at mid-century, expanded the authority of its superintendent, codified an expanded bureaucracy in 1883, and persisted in that direction until 1913 when Ellwood Cubberly found the system incredibly rigid and virtually devoid of educative functions. Still the goddess of efficiency so beguiled educators in American cities that few resisted her charms. Nor, apparently, did they care to.[12]

Moreover, rural schools also fell under the spell. From 1875 onward, rural administrators, though they might reject almost anything else smacking of urbanism, succumbed to the lure of the cities' school system, just as urban attractions were drawing away their populations, their teachers, and even their resources. Country school officials attempted, effectively in many cases, to superimpose urban patterns of organization, from graded schools through expert superintending officers, upon the rural school in order to achieve efficiency, economy, and effectiveness. Unification, supervision, division of function, and systematic organization as practiced in the city seemed to promise remedies for the perplexities of scattered populations, lack of coordination between political and educational boundaries and units, uninspired nonprofessional school officers, disagreement over educational principles, dwindling economic resources, and the paucity of qualified teachers. Indeed, rural educators even accepted the expedient of providing transportation for students in order to unify remote districts and make them more amenable to urban-style solutions.[13]

Although history failed to confirm rural educators' faith in organization, the attempt to apply the urban model to the problems of the country school does illustrate the appeal, pervasiveness, and vitality of the bureaucratic ideal in the Gilded Age. Moreover, such efforts, successful or not, tended to harden and render inflexible still another segment of the American public educational structure.[14]

In some respects, the effort to reform the structure of urban school systems did succeed. Establishment of a hierarchical bureaucracy with a virtually autonomous educational expert at its apex, division of function between a legislative school board and an executive superintendent and among specialized administrative assistants, extension of standardization in operational procedures, and fixing the graded form upon the school itself all contributed to a rationalized, efficient operation. However, there were also misgivings, even among those responsible for the development of the system. Commissioner of Education John Eaton summarized negative characteristics which would become apparent in the twentieth century when he wrote in 1882:

As great centres of wealth and population, cities . . . offer great advantages for the work of public education. At the same time, the magnitude of the undertaking . . . calls for the most thorough organization, and organization implies what is often termed machinery. Machinery—schemes, regulations, tests, tabulated representation, etc.—has, it is well known, an undue influence over minds of a certain order. To them, routine is progress, and they believe in nothing that cannot be formally reported. Education becomes mechanical and fruitless when such men have authority to order its conduct or pass final judgment on its results.[15]

Laymen shared Eaton's apprehension. "Huge educational machines," wrote Charles Francis Adams, Jr., "are organized . . . as a combination of the cotton mill and the railroad with the model of the state prison," and the vogues of superintendency and evolutionary thought produced nothing but mechanical schools in American cities. Even the indomitable educational bureaucrat William H. Maxwell of Brooklyn and New York City recognized that the process might reach a point of diminishing returns by removing competent teachers from classrooms, raising the status of administrators, creating dissension in the teaching ranks, overdividing responsibility, allotting too much time to the routine of examining teachers and students, and increasing costs to provide for administrative personnel. Although Maxwell's assessment was almost prophetic, during his superintendency Brooklyn maintained a ratio of one administrator or supervisor for every eleven teachers, and Maxwell himself was destined to head the colossus of all urban school bureaucracies, the Greater New York City district created in 1896. Despite awareness of inherent dangers, urban administrators like Maxwell committed themselves to the twin concepts of scientific management and bureaucratic organization in city schools—principles that meant more authority to the superintendent, more restrictions upon the teacher, less individualism for the student, and ultimately less interaction with the community.[16]

For the teacher, whether competent and professionally trained or not, the ever-watchful eye of the supervisor and a rigidly prescribed course of study precluded innovation, discouraged creativity, and compelled conformity to the rules of the system. As Andrew S. Draper of New York City observed, rules had to be "adapted not only to the best, but to the worst of teachers" and consequently circumscribed the former as closely as the latter. For the student, results were similar. In 1894 Superintendent James M. Greenwood of Kansas City described lessons "well adapted to illustrate the method in vogue in good schools in this country," and took evident pride in the rote, mechanical system of education his examples demonstrated. Students memorized a multitude of facts and fed their catechisms back to teachers with little regard for meaning or application. And as an educator of considerable stature among his peers, Greenwood unquestionably spoke for the majority of his colleagues in his assessment of good education. So widely accepted was the desire for organization and uniformity that it pressed both teachers and students into uncompromising molds and stifled nearly all individualism. Indeed, at least one city system achieved the penultimate of order; the Portland superintendent, merely by turning to the appropriate page in a curriculum guide, could determine the lesson in progress in any given grade at any moment of any day. Such conditions, whether educators intended it or not, tended to stultify education, solidify social classes, and inhibit the kind of mobility public schools were intended to promote.[17]

Nevertheless, educators in the Gilded Age generally accepted the educational machinery and believed with John D. Philbrick that

it is obviously impossible to make the so-called machine or organization too perfect; for it is certainly impossible to adapt means to ends too well. The plain fact is that the great and undisputed success of our great city systems is the result of their good organization.

It is clear in retrospect that Philbrick was far too sanguine in his evaluation of the "success of our great city systems." Yet it is equally apparent that most of his colleagues shared his optimistic view and opted to make the school a replica of existing industrial bureaucratic society, not an instrument for change, and they elected to perfect the machine.[18]

Why urban educators, men of intelligence, sensitivity, and discrimination, chose bureaucratic organization and the educational machine to solve problems of the city schools is not precisely clear. Yet some reasonably sound judgments may be made. The most apparent explanation is the urban impact itself. As one observer commented in retrospect:

It is because economic and social conditions have arisen—conditions that a half century past were entirely unknown and almost unthinkable—that increased emphasis is placed upon the organization and conduct of the metropolitan school district. These conditions, growing out of a civilization complex and many sided, demand increased efficiency, more serviceable output, and higher moral standards.

New urban conditions bearing directly on the school included the decline in the nature and relationships of the family unit, political and social unrest growing out of economic conditions, assimilation of foreign elements, care required by delinquents and defectives, difficulties in furnishing students with transportation, books, and supplies, and the cities' legal and fiscal complexities.[19]

Such conditions, born with astonishing swiftness, existed in abundance in the cities of the late 1800s and impelled educators to substitute order for the apparent chaos and disintegration of urban life, but experience provided few models upon which to proceed. And organization and centralization of control probably seemed to furnish the most direct, rapid, and concrete means toward the desired order. Such a simple explanation is not wholly satisfactory, however, for educators recognized the dangers implicit in centralization. They were men of acumen and obvious sincerity, and they were conscious of alternate approaches to the reformation of the school and society. Furthermore, they did not initially commit themselves to any one course of action; for no such course existed in educational theory until schoolmen devised it. Nor did the presence of urban school problems dictate the nature of the solution. Nevertheless, by the turn of the century a nearly universally accepted mode for dealing with the difficulties of the urban school had developed, and it became the equally accepted pattern for urban school organization throughout the nation.

It is certainly no coincidence—though the influence often is subtle—that many aspects of that organizational pattern are included in the various evolutionary theories which permeated the thought of the Gilded Age. Whether deriving from Charles Darwin, Herbert Spencer, William Graham Sumner, or even August Comte, such theories stressed social and political development from the simple to the complex, increasing diversity and specialization, the indisputable necessity of division of function, and, as an inevitable corollary, the evolutionary emergence of a higher individual—the expert. Moreover, directed by immutable natural laws, society itself followed an appointed progressive course from an uncomplicated pastoral stage to a complex industrial level. Educators, like many of their contemporaries, saw in such theories a description of events they were in fact witnessing, not only in the nation but also in the city and in the urban school itself. Indeed, some found in Herbert Spencer's doctrines "the guiding thread that shall lead us through the labyrinth" of a rapidly changing society.[20]

For most educators, however, commitment to Spencer's thought remained less explicit. Yet it was implicit in the ideas of most, and in their discussions of the necessity for organization, efficiency, and expert management in the public schools. The evolutionist terminology—division of function, specialization, hierarchical organization, and the assumption that "higher individuals" should manage affairs—was frequently a component of the pedagogues' rhetoric. So, too, was the comfortable—and perhaps comforting—assumption that once set in motion according to the laws of nature, the wheels of progress turned, making both social and educational progress inevitable. At the close of the century Nicholas Murray Butler observed that "The two principles of evolution and individualism viewed in the light of the history of civilization . . . determine the status of education," and what had evolved at the institutional level, to the satisfaction of most educators, was a struct red hierarchical system which seemed to confirm the Spencerian analysis. Meanwhile, William Torrey Harris arrived at approximately the same comfortable positivist position by the Hegelian rather than the Spencerian route and on the basis of a firm faith in the beneficence of technological progress.[21]

Even more subtle than the influence of evolutionist thought—but no less significant—was the apparent ascendancy of the methods and ideologies of business and industry. It has already been seen that at the functional level, educators readily accepted the metaphor of the machine to describe city school systems. Moreover, despite a certain insecurity concerning modern society and the social changes resulting from industrialization, schoolmen were by and large confident that technology ultimately would bring progress, rejuvenate society, and heal its infirmities. Still more important, however, for the emergence of bureaucracy in the urban school was the influence of business and industry at the structural level. For both in business and in industry, organization and management ostensibly brought order out of chaos. Men such as Carnegie, Rockefeller, Vanderbilt, and Morgan rationalized production, transportation, and finance and made them not only efficient but also profitable. Consequently, as Frederic C. Howe commented in 1906, "The inspiration of early [municipal] reform movements was a desire for a business men's government."[22] The same lesson can hardly have been lost on the nation's educators.

Indeed, it was not. The business successes of the era indirectly shaped both the content and form of urban education. Jane Addams observed in 1897 that the business community did not overtly press public education to produce a crop of trained clerks and workers ready for employment. It was simply unnecessary. As early as 1874, educators had committed the schools to the preservation of the traditional values of punctuality, regularity, attention, silence, and respect for property with explicit emphasis upon their new application in an industrial and commercial society.[23] Moreover, despite the absence of direct pressure, educators throughout the era demonstrated responsiveness to the business community's needs by changing curricular content in the direction of manual and industrial training, business education, commercial courses, and the like, and by reorienting traditional subjects to conform to business and industrial needs.

Had there been extensive pressure from the business community, the alterations would have been less significant. Even without such direct influence, urban educational leaders apparently absorbed many of the values and attitudes of the businessman, and some, at least, began to think of themselves less as educators than as school executives. We do not know whether such self-evaluation anticipated or followed from the bureaucratic restructuring of the city school. But, undoubtedly, urban schoolmen observed advantages resulting from organization, centralization, management, and authority and were eager to apply those principles to the city school. Nor is it likely that they overlooked the similarity between the conditions leading to the consolidation of industry and their own practical problems. The economic climate of the Gilded Age made it but a short step to the conviction that the very attributes that made a successful businessman or business organization were also requisites for the efficient management of urban school systems.[24]

Moreover, urban school administrators assumed not only the ideology and methods of the business executive, but even his manner and dress. Aaron Gove of Denver, for example, arrived at the 1884 NEA Convention driving an ornate buggy drawn by a high-stepping sorrel. According to an observer, Gove was

a gentleman . . . with dark eyes and a heavy dark mustache that might have been dyed, . . . dressed in an elegant white wool suit cut Prince Albert style, with a white stovepipe hat tilted jauntily over one eye, . . . smoking a long cigar.

Two other "well-dressed, fine looking men, with iron gray hair and neatly trimmed beards, were seen lying in the shade on the lawn, smoking cigars," and these were Superintendents John Hancock of Toledo and Andrew J. Rickoff of Yonkers. The descriptions hardly suggest the traditional schoolmaster, and such was the subtle but pervasive—and persuasive—influence of the business world upon the educational "man of affairs" that he could no longer be simply a master teacher or even think of himself as such. Necessity and choice had made him an administrator, competent in economics, law, legislation, and the principles of organization and management.[25] There is, however, little indication that he found the change unwelcome. Indeed, the urban conditions of the Gilded Age undoubtedly made the change seem not only necessary but also quite natural.

It would be too facile a judgment to insist that the influence of either business ideology or evolutionary philosophy was sufficient of itself to cause educators and municipal reformers to accept the bureaucratic system as their principal weapon in the fight to reform the city and the urban school. Yet it is not too much to argue that both concepts facilitated the decision to fasten that system and all of its consequences upon the schools of American cities for generations. The city itself, however, provided at least one more condition that made centralization seem the surest solution to urban school problems. James Bryce described it as the major flaw in democracy in the United States: municipal politics.

4

Municipal Politics and the Public School

If there was one thing more than another that I desired to keep absolutely aloof from politics, it was the conduct of the city public schools.
—Christopher A. Buckley

When San Francisco's Democratic "Blind Boss" of the 1880s, Christopher Augustine Buckley, vowed emphatically in his memoirs that he had kept the operation of the city public schools "absolutely aloof from politics," he was being less than candid. Throughout his tenure as political chieftain, as well as in preceding and subsequent decades, partisanship penetrated the San Francisco school system, much to the dismay of local educators and reformers. It was, however, not a situation unique to the Pacific Coast city. Indeed, educational leaders across the nation found that in urban centers "all the natural enemies of sound administration scent plenty of plunder" in the potential for graft and patronage grabs which the schools offered, and that knowledge disturbed them profoundly. The premise that schools, though public and democratic, ought not to be "political" had persisted in popular and educational thought since Horace Mann's time. In the late 1800s, however, the assumption evolved into a clearly defined and universally pursued goal of educational and municipal reform, articulated as the belief that "the idea of representing nationalities, or localities, or peculiarities of interest [in the conduct of the city schools] . . . is an erroneous idea, and is amenable to charges of inefficiency."[1]

Indeed, that belief became an article of faith in the rhetoric and literature of reform. "Politics"—consistently a negative term equated with corruption—constituted an unacceptable element in the management of urban school affairs and, by extension, in the operation of cities themselves. But it is not surprising that politics should acquire a pejorative connotation in the educators' lexicon. Antiquated school systems, more appropriate to the midcentury walking city than to the emerging and expanding metropolis, encouraged political involvement. Perhaps they even necessitated it, since the political structures of urban public education, like those of municipal machines and of the cities themselves, remained firmly rooted in the partisanship of city wards.

Usually created in an earlier generation when both cities and their educational needs were significantly less complex, late nineteenth-century school systems did encourage political manipulations, frequently of the worst sort. Typically, voters in individual wards elected a local school board. The basic element in the educational hierarchy, ward school committees, exercised broad and substantial powers which belied their rank: hiring and promoting teachers and other school employees, defining curricula, designating school location and supervising their construction and maintenance, prescribing pedagogical methods, and awarding contracts for supplies and services. Ward committees in many cities, either by election or appointment, delegated representatives to citywide school boards charged with more general authority: certificating teachers, overseeing general school operations, granting imprimatur to ward committee actions, and selecting city school administrators, including a superintendent when that official was not chosen at a municipal election. In most cities, prior to turn-of-the-century reforms, superintendents performed strictly limited functions: supervising and training teachers, recommending policy, and executing board-approved actions. Finally, and perhaps of greatest significance, partisan municipal conventions nominated candidates for virtually every school office.[2] To be sure, cities of nearly endless variety produced equally numerous modifications and adaptations of the system. Nevertheless, in the late 1800s, nearly every American city utilized a decentralized plan of school organization grounded firmly in local partisan politics and vesting diffused authority in numerous nonprofessional elective boards and officials. As a consequence, irresponsibility, confusion, and petty corruption frequently characterized the operation of urban public education.

Professional educators—especially higher echelon administrators—denounced the system, the political involvement inherent in it, and the host of evils attributable to politics. Dominance by supposedly venal and ignorant ward trustees produced a multitude of opportunities for partisan chicanery, not a sound basis for educational efficiency. Positions on ward and city school boards provided access to higher office, not occasions for service to the schools, and attracted petty politicos—and some not so petty—not the best men in the community. Ward heelers, local school committees, city boards of education, and even superintendents could manipulate the educational system and subvert its lofty and idealistic goals. Consequently ,reformist educators in late nineteenth-century cities harbored little confidence in the effectiveness of public school systems, in the integrity of the officials who managed them, or in the wisdom and honesty of the voters who elected them. Deficiencies in education could be traced directly to political involvement, but only rarely—and this is a most significant point—did the rhetoric of urban educational reform in the Gilded Age distinguish between the legitimate ends of politics in the city and politics as corruption.[3]

Without question, minor corruption did persist and permeate entire educational structures. Using patronage and favoritism, both ward and citywide school boards consistently exploited their powers not only for partisan purposes but also for personal, professional, social, and commercial gain. Indeed, in 1898 one city superintendent complained that in his twenty-year experience he "never had a school committee which could be relied upon to vote for . . . the interests of the schools, regardless of 'pulls.' " School trustees filled positions from superintendent to janitor on the basis of the number of voters in the applicant's family, potential business or social benefits, religious affiliations, or possibly a salary kickback, rather than on the basis of ability. In more than one city, classrooms became a form of outdoor relief, "very proper place[s] to pension indigent gentlewomen," among others. A friend at court in the person of a board member, a precinct captain, or even the local pastor constituted the most frequent basis for such employment. In addition to such pressures, publishers' agents, contractors, stationers, and numerous other enterprises seeking the business of the city schools plied both ward and central board members with gifts, favors, political contributions, or even outright bribes. Despite the relatively minor material considerations involved in such transactions, educators deplored them and universally attributed them to "political tricksters who give positions to incompetent teachers . . . [and] steal from defenseless children."[4] Political pettifogging not only violated public and personal morality but also created unbusinesslike confusion, waste, and inefficiency in the public schools, the cardinal sins in the educators' Decalogue.

In cities across the nation, educators found such political intrusions rampant, destructive, and culpable, and schoolmen reacted against them, often in concert with local good-government movements with which they shared not only timing but also ideology. Educators' goals, like those of municipal reform, typically involved structural change: the reorganization of city public school systems in order to centralize authority, the separation of education from partisan politics by taking it out of the hands of "ignorant, selfish, or unprincipled officials" and voters, and the creation of businesslike, professional, and above all efficient systems of school management.[5]

Indeed, the history of virtually any major city during the closing quarter of the century would provide useful insights into the response to politics as a factor in the emergence of modern bureaucratic urban school systems. From coast to coast, concerted efforts modified educational structures with the explicit purpose of divorcing schools from partisanship. However, developments in San Francisco hold particular interest. Most obviously, as in many other urban centers, these developments furnish concrete examples of the kind of political infiltration, reformist response, and long-range consequences which typify municipal educational reform in the Gilded Age. But in other ways, the city of San Francisco has been considered outside the mainstream of American urban history. It was a young city, incorporated not fifty years by the turn of the century. Moreover, neither heavy industrialization nor impaction by a single immigrant group characterized its economic and social conditions. Finally, its political development usually has not been regarded as typical of the evolution of American municipalities. Despite apparent uniqueness, however, the city's experience with its schools was, in fact, similar to the pattern in other urban centers across the nation. And it is this combination of uniqueness and similarity that renders the San Francisco experience historically revealing.

Although the city's plan of school organization was not entirely typical, neither was it atypical. San Francisco had no ward-level school boards. However, according to the Consolidation Act of 1856 under which the city was governed until 1898, responsibility for public education devolved upon a biennially-elected Board of School Directors, consisting of one member from each of the city's twelve wards, and an elected superintendent of schools charged with serving as secretary to the board, executing board decisions, visiting each school in the city at least quarterly, and very little else.[6] With school officials nominated at local party conventions and chosen at municipal elections, it is unsurprising that politics provided the basis for public school operation in San Francisco almost from the beginning of the city's history or that the very conditions educators deplored came to prevail.

Patronage persisted as the most consistently condemned offense against sound education. Until 1876 school directors appointed teachers for only a single year, precipitating annual ordeals of reexamination and unseemly scrambles for positions. Few applicants failed to pass purposely simple examinations, however, and with patronage informally shared among the directors, influence, rather than competence became the criterion for appointment. Initially, "pulls" apparently involved favors, friendship, or economic need rather than cash or votes; nevertheless, efforts to alter the system began early. In 1869 city officials secured state legislation granting the mayor authority to appoint a superintendent, but shifts in partisan strength brought almost immediate repeal. Three years later, a law requiring a teaching certificate as qualification for the city superintendency suffered a similar fate. And in 1876 an amendment to the Consolidation Act eliminated annual appointments and made teacher tenure contingent upon "competency and good behavior." But nothing in the operation of San Francisco schools changed perceptibly.[7]

Despite legalistic manipulations, the educational system remained an essentially political organism, and by 1878 the process of appointing teachers clearly involved more than mere favoritism. In order to substantiate suspected corruption, the San Francisco *Evening Bulletin* purchased and published annual certification examinations. Along with other local journals, the paper raised questions of leaks, influence, bribery, and political perfidy in its exposé. To be sure, subsequent investigation found that examinations were sold (it was never quite clear by whom) and implicated officials of the State Department of Public Instruction which formulated the tests and the U. S. Post Office which conveyed them to the city. But no major upheaval ensued from the "great school scandal" of 1878, possibly because school directors investigated themselves. The furor did little to alter conditions. Nor did a new state constitution accomplish more when in 1879 it augmented local control over teacher hiring and certification and thereby expanded opportunity for partisan incursions. A year later, the city superintendent would reiterate the increasingly familiar complaint: "pleas of poverty, orphanage, religious and social ties, political services—past or to come—

are showered upon the directors," influencing the award of positions and contracts alike.[8] What is more, Chris Buckley would soon turn haphazard grafting into a system which advocates of municipal efficiency might well envy.

As a Republican, Buckley had learned the art of politics in San Francisco and Vallejo saloons in the 1860s but the decline of the Democratic party in the former city provided his real opportunity in the 1870s. Buckley switched his allegiance, rebuilt the San Francisco Democracy, and by 1882 established himself as undisputed master of the party, despite his blindness. Employing the boss's traditional techniques—association with business interests and the underworld, controlling local primary elections, and distributing patronage and social services—the Blind Boss and his followers (called "Lambs" by a hostile press) established and maintained control over the city's functions, including its educational system. With over 700 employees—more than all other city agencies combined—the school department provided numerous sources of patronage and opportunities for pulling and plundering. Positions in the system could reward political service, or the consideration might be cash. Although Buckley himself professed innocence, teaching positions in San Francisco sold for up to $200, payable to an intermediary, to a school director, or into political coffers. Moreover, in order to circumvent the 1876 law abolishing annual teacher appointment, Buckley's school directors created a new official, the "Inspecting Teacher," whose negative evaluation alone constituted grounds for dismissal—and a vacancy to be filled for funds or favors.[9] More simply, directors could create and fill teaching positions at will.

Following the 1882 Buckley sweep of municipal elections, outgoing Republican school directors appointed a host of new teachers and administrators as a parting gesture, unperturbed by the fact that one-third of the school year had already elapsed. Not to be outdone, the Buckley board, at its initial meeting, swept away the school system's entire clerical and custodial staff, bringing "sorrow to a score of Republican hearts," and proceeded to fill the places with more worthy and congenial Democrats. The directors' action did not go entirely without challenge, however; the newly-elected superintendent registered a public but rather timid protest, touching off a running dispute with the board, and one director tendered his resignation, only to recant after overnight reconsideration.[10]

Obviously, neither the board's tactics nor the internecine conflict generated predicted educational or economic stability and efficiency for the city's schools in the Buckley era. Moreover, neither Buckley's grand jury indictment in 1891 nor the subsequent dispersal of his Lambs terminated school politics in San Francisco. Throughout the subsequent regime of Buckley's Republican counterpart, Martin Kelly, complaints about school operation and the department's political nature remained both constant and consistent: patronage, secret board meetings, fiscal deficits, incompetence, favoritism, and dilapidated facilities. Politics remained firmly entrenched in the school system, patronage and favors guided the directors' exercise of their duties, and ineffective teaching by incompetent teachers in inadequate school facilities constituted the inevitable result. Bosses and their organizations made politics an integral part of public education and reaped substantial personal and organizational profits in the process. School department jobs could be utilized to assist the needy, reward the loyal, or provide avenues of upward mobility, as well as to fill pockets and campaign chests. Contracts for school buildings, supplies, and a multitude of services could be awarded or expedited, winning not only loyalty but also contributions from businessmen.[11]

All of this was quasi-legal at best or strictly illegal at worst; yet conditions bred by rapid urbanization and by antiquated political and school systems made it possible if not inevitable. According to one contemporary observer:

The defects of the laws of San Francisco originated in attempts to adapt to a metropolitan city of 350,000 a charter which was made for a town of 40,000, and in the fact that amendments extending over forty years had so confused matters that it was difficult to facilitate government.[12]

As appropriate to school operations as to the general management of the city, the comment described conditions in dozens of cities. Into the vacuum and confusion created by defective legal systems and social turmoil stepped the political bosses, astute organizers who built efficient and businesslike systems of control upon weaknesses inherent in the municipal legal structures and in urban society itself.

What politicos found efficient and businesslike, however, repelled the better citizens of American cities including San Francisco, where four charter revision drives, all including school reform provisions, failed between 1880 and 1896. In 1897 Mayor James D. Phelan headed a fifth effort involving 1,000 members of the Merchants Association, the Local Council of Women, the San Francisco Committee of 100, most of the city's editors and clergymen, and a host of its leading citizens. And a reform victory rewarded their efforts when voters approved a new city charter in 1898. Educational provisions of the charter—aiming at efficiency, businesslike management, professionalism, and the separation of school affairs from local politics—institutionalized reformist ideals. A paid, four-member bipartisan Board of School Directors, appointed by the mayor to staggered four-year terms, constituted the most notable departure and clearly reflected reformers' goals. The superintendent, popularly elected to a four-year term, received expanded authority including power to select four assistants at terms and salaries to be determined by the board, and retained sole responsibility for all personnel matters, especially hiring, certificating, and promoting teachers. Between the executive authority of the superintendent and the legislative responsibility of the directors, the charter drew clear lines of demarcation and circumscription.[13]

Both the first superintendent under the new system and the first president of the newly appointed board had been active in the charter movement, and like other San Franciscans, they anticipated significant progress in the function of the city schools. The San Francisco *Chronicle,* itself a staunch charter advocate, predicted "rapid advancement and marked improvement in the efficiency of the School Department," and the board president added:

Our material advantage will be that the board of education will be a continuous body, and this fact will be conducive to a uniform system of education. The new board of education is probably the only paid board in the country, and it devolves upon us to show that a paid [nonpolitical] board can be of more success than an unpaid board.

The new body would be efficient, professional, and businesslike; therefore, it would be above politics and hence more effective in the discharge of its duties.[14]

Despite reformers' high expectations, structural changes resulted in neither harmony nor freedom from politics. At its initial meeting, the new board quarreled with the superintendent over appointments, terms, and salaries of assistant superintendents, thereby opening a breach which intensified. Disappointed editors exacerbated the conflict, as did the vocal discontent of teachers who had not participated in devising the new system and who regarded the board's economy drive —quite rightly—as a threat to their positions. But if such minor immediate clashes did not augur well for success, subsequent developments revealed the real weaknesses of structural reform. In 1901 Boss Abe Ruef's Union Labor party swept municipal elections and carried Eugene Schmitz into the office of mayor. Subsequently, Schmitz's crony Alfred Roncovieri took a seat on the board of education and in 1904 became the board's president. A year later, Ruef's brother-in-law became a board member, and simultaneously Roncovieri began a seventeen-year tenure as superintendent of schools, the longest in the city's history.[15]

This does not necessarily imply corruption on the part of either; however, it does suggest emphatically that politics, even as reformers defined it, remained intimately involved in city school management. Moreover, the events dramatically illustrate a defect in the concept of structural change, which reformers apparently chose to ignore: for good or ill, centralized authority and appointive power vested in fewer hands could easily expand the potential for political involvement. Control of the mayor's office now meant de facto control of the school board as well, without the involvement of any other civic agency or even the popular will. Still, when the new system failed to produce the desired results, San Francisco reformers advocated eliminating even the election of the superintendent, allowing the board to fill the office by appointment and thus extending the mayor's direct and indirect control over school affairs.[16] Commitment to centralization apparently obscured some of its inherent flaws.

Had developments in San Francisco been unique, they would be significant nonetheless. However, both contemporary accounts and recent historical scholarship indicate that in cities across the nation similar conditions in urban school politics precipitated analogous responses by concerned educators. Both motivations and consequences are sufficiently comparable to suggest a nationwide pattern. For example, in the first true American metropolis, New York City, the school system had long been the bailiwick of Tammany Hall politicos. That city's unwieldy twenty-one-member central board, weak superintendency, and numerous ward committees made graft and petty corruption endemic in school operation. Despite reformers' legalistic and institutional tinkering dating from the School Law of 1873, already inefficient school conditions continued to deteriorate until even the distribution of ward committees bore no resemblance to schools or populations. By 1895, for example, the four-member Third Ward School Committee reported paying a teacher's salary, although there were neither schools nor children in the district. More seriously, bribery and the use of patronage in appointing teachers and other school employees and in awarding contracts remained both common and blatant.

In 1896 reformist response, led principally by Elihu Root and President Nicholas Murray Butler of Columbia University Teachers' College, secured a "Greater City" school law uniting jurisdiction over the educational systems of all boroughs under a single authority. The new law eliminated ward committees, reduced the size of the city school board and made it appointive; it also provided for an appointed superintendent and twenty assistants. Results resembled those in San Francisco. Various groups—teachers, advocates of pluralism, politicians, and a significant element of the public at large—resented the implications of bureaucratic reorganization and expressed disfavor by supporting Tammany's recurrent "To Hell with Reform" campaigns. As in San Francisco, the resultant capture of the municipal government now meant augmented and even more lucrative possibilities for patronage, pulls, and plunder in the city schools.[17]

Bostonians, too, sought to consolidate control over a school system that had eliminated ward representation as early as 1876. There, however, overlapping jurisdictions, inefficiency, and patronage involving ethnic, religious, social, and political ties continued to influence the selection of teachers, appointment of administrators, awarding of contracts, and the efficiency of education into the 1890s. Confusion persisted, characterized by occasionally comic episodes such as the year-long penmanship controversy when the school board first adopted the diagonal system for handwriting instruction, then reversed itself in favor of the vertical method, still later ruled that individual schools might experiment with both, and finally adopted the vertical system but approved textbooks for the diagonal. In 1894, as a result of such gyrations, leading citizens and educators mounted a reform campaign based upon typical principles: centralization, efficiency, professionalism, bureaucratic organization, and an appointive board of education. To be sure, politics and religion combined to prevent success of Yankee-Protestant-Republican reform in Irish-Catholic-Democratic Boston. Nevertheless, school reformers did manage to institutionalize portions of their objectives by 1898. More significantly, motivations for reform and the nature of measures attempted or implemented to remedy deficiencies in Boston closely resembled reformist programs in other cities, particularly in the desire to circumscribe politics.[18]

Indeed, though degrees of success varied, similar conditions and patterns of response prevailed across the nation in the 1890s. Philadelphia's 36-member, ward-based board of education and 36-ward-level school committees kept teachers subject to the authority of 533 individuals in overlapping jurisdictions, and the city's educational system was embroiled in political strife. Despite reformers' decade-long struggle to centralize control, eliminate politics, and impose bureaucratic forms of management—and the conviction of several ward trustees on charges of extortion—Philadelphia schools remained intensely political institutions, the ultimate contradiction to the gospel of educational efficiency. Nor were similar reform efforts more successful in Baltimore. Politics kept the schools in perpetual chaos through the city council's authority to appoint a twenty-two-member board of school commissioners and the latter body's total control over all aspects of the school system, including employment and contracts. The response was typical. A good-government movement secured a new city charter in 1898, eliminated ward representation, reduced school board size, and expanded the superintendent's authority. Still, school problems remained and ultimately involved teacher and civic associations, publishers' agents, the trial and dismissal of a nationally known superintendent, and an investigation by the U.S. Bureau of Education.[19]

Analogous patterns of reformists response to political involvement evolved in many American cities in the 1890s: Chicago, St. Louis, Cleveland, Toledo, Cincinnati, Denver, Milwaukee, and Portland, among others. Indeed, the developments are more than analogous; in certain respects they are nearly identical. To be sure, reformers devised specific programs and institutions appropriate to their individual cities, degrees of success varied widely, and they occasionally even compromised with local bosses.[20] However, the inherent consistency among ideologies involved in reformist responses implies the emergence of a new and broad consensus concerning the nature of effective school systems. That set of ideas, at the heart of which was a deep and abiding hostility toward "politics," shaped modern, bureaucratically organized urban educational institutions.

Scholarly research has placed corruption and reform among the most familiar aspects of the history of American cities in the late 1800s. Historians and political scientists have demonstrated conclusively that bossism and machine politics entrenched themselves in defective and frequently impotent municipal governmental structures and that upper-and middle-class reform movements—through such agencies as the National Municipal League, local good-government movements, various committees of 100 (more or less), and other civic groups—influenced modern municipal institutions, including the now familiar multitude of combinations and variations of the commission, city manager, and mayor-council forms of city government. Yet little has been said about similar developments or their implications in urban education, despite a significant body of evidence which points not only to widespread corruption but also to the deep conviction among educational leaders that the "natural enemies" of effective schools—most frequently identified as local politicians —eagerly capitalized upon weaknesses inherent in archaic school systems, creating or magnifying a host of problems: inefficiency, unbusinesslike management, and a dearth of men of integrity willing to involve themselves in school affairs. All of these defects could be traced to a single source: "politics."[21]

Emergence of educational bureaucracies cannot, of course, be attributed solely to educators' antipathy toward politics. The desire to establish businesslike and efficient systems of management, the conception of education as an instrument of social control, and impulses toward professionalism and modernism all contributed toward that end. Still, hostility toward politics rarely remained far below the surface in educators' rhetoric, ideology, or analysis of city school problems. Inefficiency—culpable in itself—could be attributed to political incursions, which resulted in corruption of the schools and also of civic morality. Similarly, the deep involvement of patronage in the distribution of teaching positions inhibited professionalism and further diminished educational effectiveness. Finally, awarding contracts for buildings, materials, textbooks, and services depended upon political pulls or plunder and made economy in school operation virtually impossible. Prescribed remedies likewise implied hostility to politics: reducing or eliminating ward school representation on boards, circumscribing school board authority, appointing—rather than electing—both board members and professional administrators, and augmenting administrative authority.

All of these proposals tended toward a divorce of school affairs not only from partisan politics but also from popular participation and toward a greater centralization of authority. Nevertheless, a plea for bureaucratic organization accompanied virtually every exposé of politics, pulls, and plunder in late nineteenth-century urban school systems. Moreover, educators and reformers made personal ideologies and motivations apparent. While articulating commitment to efficient, businesslike, and effective schools, they simultaneously expressed agreement with E. L. Godkin that the "large body of political heathen," native and immigrant alike, inhabiting American cities could not be trusted with governing them. Nor should they be involved in school affairs. Educators eschewed pluralism, mistrusted the politics of the masses, and presumed that appointive officials were necessarily less corruptible than elective ones. Consequently, objectives entailed the organization of educational structures with limited popular influence, authority and jurisdiction over schools being delegated to reliable citizens and experts who presumably would be above politics.[22]

As a result of such attitudes, educators failed to secure a broad base of support for their programs. Indeed, they rarely made the attempt. Elitism and paternalism consistently characterized conceptions of the political process and perhaps even limited faith in democracy itself. Superintendent Andrew S. Draper of Cleveland well may have captured reformist attitudes when he wrote:

As it becomes more and more imperative to have strong, experienced men and honest men to manage the business of great cities, it also becomes, for obvious reasons, more and more difficult to secure them on the basis of unrestricted suffrage. . . . The fact that [public officials] . . . are elected at a general city election is unfortunate.[23]

Although Draper did not enumerate the obvious reasons, his meaning is clear. Like many other reformers, he questioned the ability of popular judgment to select superior men and assumed that it was in fact possible and desirable to eliminate politics from the operation of public schools through the centralization of control in bureaucratic systems of management.

In its hostility to politics, educational reform bore a close resemblance to concurrent good-government and charter-revision movements, and it also shared an oversight with them: the possibility that centralized systems could provide political machines with even greater opportunity and thus become something less than effective instruments for permanent or positive change. Indeed, both movements, though political themselves, equated politics with corruption, and both attempted to abolish politics, "the idea of representing nationalities, or localities, or peculiarities of interest," from municipal affairs—a principle applied to no other level of government in the nation. Moreover, the ideologies of both movements became institutionalized at the national level through such agencies as the National Municipal League, on the one hand, and the NEA Department of Superintendence, on the other. Finally, the consensus that emerged in both movements is important. Like civic reformers who concentrated on revising charters, educational reformers focused their efforts upon altering the structural aspects of city school systems and in the process frequently made the system's function—education—subordinate to its organizational framework.[24]

When centralized and bureaucratic educational systems failed to operate as anticipated or succumbed to reasserted political influences, educators attributed failure neither to the

concept of centralization nor to fallacies in their own attitudes concerning the nature of politics. Instead, they charged
it to the ignorance of the masses, who continued to participate
in the political process, and to insufficient centralization of
authority. Therefore, educators attempted to treat each new
symptom of infirmity in city school systems with increased
doses of the same medicine. Thus, through persistent hostility
to politics and commitment to bureaucratic operational procedures, reformers established a pattern for city schools,
which became not only nationalized and institutionalized but
also self-perpetuating. The structures they created would become, like many other urban institutions, increasingly rigid
and decreasingly sensitive to social, economic, and ethno-
demographic conditions in American cities. Indeed, bureaucracy eliminated politics of one sort only to substitute another.
In the process, it tended to diminish the responsiveness of
public education to the people for whom it theoretically existed.

The weaknesses of politics in the cities of the Gilded Age
are, to be sure, all too apparent. Nevertheless, politics had
forced at least some school officials to respond to a constituency, a point reformers consistently ignored. Even that tenuous
connection began to disappear with the introduction of supposedly apolitical school bureaucracies at the turn of the
century. As one of Chris Buckley's San Francisco contemporaries assessed the matter:

The [political] boss was at least a real man, a warm-blooded
verterbrate [sic]. To that extent he was better than a silent,
unseen, underground machine. . . . The people knew where to
find him, knew how to discipline him when occasion arose.[25]

Much the same might be said of the involvement of politics
in late nineteenth-century urban education. Indeed, it may not
be too much to suggest that many current educational problems in American cities have substantial roots in the ideologies
of antipolitical reform movements of the Gilded Age.

5

Impulses and Attitudes of Educational Reform

The wheels of Progress can no more stop than the earth can stand still.
　　　　　　　　　　　　—William H. Maxwell

Educational reformers in the cities of the Gilded Age shared numerous attitudes, impulses, and habits of thought—including their common antipathy toward politics, their nearly unanimous commitment to centralization of authority, and their collective urge to rejuvenate society through the medium of the public school—which united them in a common cause. The sources of their consensus, however, remain less distinct than the ideas themselves. The historian may be tempted to assess educators' uniformity of outlook and unity of purpose on the basis of common traits, backgrounds, and experiences, but there are dangers inherent in efforts to explain individual motives of alignment with specific movements in such a manner, particularly when reformist movements are involved. Although common origins, religious and political affiliations, or economic and social experiences may illuminate common commitments, it must be recognized that many contemporaries who shared characteristics remained alien to reform movements or even opposed them. Moreover, the very qualities which seem to identify reformers may not, in fact, substantially distinguish them from the majority of their fellow citizens. It is even more hazardous for the historian to indulge in postmortem psychoanalysis and probe personalities and experiences to discover the sources of the impulse to reform. The subjects, after all, are unavailable for examination, and the nature of the historian's training makes such analyses precarious at best. To be sure, sociological and psychological approaches have been employed with some success by scholars who attribute the abolitionist and progressivist impulse to a "status revolution" which prompted members of once dominant social classes to seek alternate channels through which to exercise influence. However, such conclusions do not necessarily apply to the analysis of all reform movements. Indeed, some challenge the entire validity of displacement analyses or object that an archetypal reformer is at best the historian's creation.[1]

To discover an archetype among Gilded Age educational reformers would require just that sort of artificial creation. For neither backgrounds nor experiences identify them as a homogeneous group or distinguish them from their contemporaries. Nor is there evidence of significant displacement. Most were born in rural settings either before or during the Civil War; yet circumstances of birth hardly differentiate them from other mature citizens among their contemporaries. Most educational reformers, professionals and laymen alike, affiliated themselves with the Republican party, hardly an uncommon attachment in post-Reconstruction America. Moreover, with the rare exception of men like Andrew S. Draper, who served a term in the New York State legislature and actively supported James G. Blaine in the presidential campaign of 1884, political activists among educators were few. Indeed, most abhorred and shunned partisanship in any form.

It is also true that more educational reformers traced their origins to New England and the Middle West than to any other section, and many—such as Draper, James M. Greenwood, Albert G. Lane, Aaron Gove, James Van Sickle, Ellwood P. Cubberly, G. Stanley Hall, John Hancock, Charles W. Eliot, William Torrey Harris, and John Lancaster Spalding—claimed ancestral roots in the colonial and pioneer stock of the seventeenth and early eighteenth centuries. But there were also those, including Joseph M. Rice, William H. Maxwell, and F. Louis Soldan, who were either descended from, or were themselves, recent immigrants. Moreover, though most were Protestants (Congregationalists, Presbyterians, and Methodists predominated), and a few such as Burke A. Hinsdale, Albert G. Lane, and G. Stanley Hall were ministers or religiously active laymen, religious affiliations neither distinguished them nor made them educational reformers, neither did the fact that most were from substantial and middle-class Anglo-Saxon origins. Most of their contemporaries had similar affiliations and origins, yet remained divorced from reform movements of any stripe. Furthermore, neither educational nor career backgrounds reveal significant similarities. Although most were college or university trained, some, including Hancock and Greenwood, were virtually self-educated. Others came to the educational profession or reform only after preparation for different careers; Draper, Edwin P. Seaver, and James C. Boykin all trained in law; Lane was a bank cashier, Rice a pediatrician, Maxwell a reporter, and Truman A. DeWeese studied medicine and was a journeyman printer. In short, educational reformers had little in their backgrounds or experience to predict their ultimate unity of purpose and ideology.[2]

There is, however, significance in their very diversity. For it suggests that an understanding of their commitment to educational reform and their conceptions of education might best be sought in the rhetoric and practices they brought to reform, rather than in more subjective evaluations of backgrounds. Diversity also underscores areas of apparent unity of thought among educators: sincere faith in education and desire to improve the school, abhorrence of partisan politics, and admiration for efficiency and organization. Finally, lack of homogeneity focuses attention not upon the reformers' past but upon actual activity, upon the nature not only of explicit pronouncements which were part of urban educational reform but also upon the ideas implicit in the tone of reformist rhetoric, and upon reformers' responses to the *Zeitgeist* of the Gilded Age.

In his 1964 analysis of elitism in municipal reform during the Progressive Era, Samuel P. Hays wrote:

it is becoming increasingly clear that ideological evidence is no safe guide to the understanding of practice, that what people thought and said about their society is not necessarily an accurate representation of what they did.[3]

Yet, as has already been seen, a consistent correlation did exist between educators' articulated ideologies and their practical implementation of principles, particularly in the realm of bureaucratic and political reorganization. Although this by no means invalidates Hays's argument that considerations other than those revealed in their pronouncements often motivated reformers, it is reasonably clear that, at least in the case of educational reform in the late 1800s, preachments and practices tended to coincide. Although remarkable diversity in experience and background typified educators, the similarity of their ideas and the consistency with which they articulated and acted upon them are equally remarkable. Politics they found repugnant, almost to a man, and they seldom hesitated to express that sentiment. Efficiency stood at the pinnacle of their scale of values and remained a central theme in the rhetoric and practice of educational reform. Businesslike organization and management occupied similarly high positions on their list of priorities. Moreover, the interrelationship perceived among those concepts was likewise consistent. In the educators' view, partisan politics was an untidy business which, by its very nature, precipitated inefficiency, repelled reputable men, facilitated misuse of authority, and corrupted democracy. Business methods, on the other hand, were neat, efficient, and proved both effective and attractive to men of high capacity. Such an appraisal, when applied to conditions in city schools, not only provided an apparently valid description of urban educational problems but also suggested obvious remedies.

Several other shared intellectual postures interacted with these understandings and with one another to lend support to educators' conclusions concerning urban school rehabilitation. Virtually every reform leader articulated or implied strongly some degree of adherence to the Social Darwinist thought which permeated the era. Most expressed an underlying fear of the masses and of popular democracy. And nearly all approached the reformist role from clearly elitist or paternalistic positions. Such concepts comprised a closely related cluster of ideas which influenced not only definitions of the school and of its functions but also understandings of the nature and limitations of educational reform.

It has already been noted that the influence of Spencerian evolutionary thought was significant in guiding attempts to restructure the urban school system in accordance with doctrines of specialization, division of function, and centralization of authority. Moreover, the creation of apparently efficient systems of school management embodying those principles worked to convince educators of the validity of William H. Maxwell's observation that "the history of evolution shows that all true reforms come slowly" and in conformity with prescribed laws. It was, furthermore, a simple matter—facilitated for some by Calvinist theology—to transfer such precepts from organizational to social understandings, to assume that Progress would eventually alleviate dislocations resulting from industrialization and urbanization, and to concede that education itself could do little to accelerate the process. Indeed, few disputed Maxwell's conclusion that evils such as "wars and pestilence and cruelty and oppression have all had their parts to play in the economy that has evolved civilization out of barbarism." None, of course, condoned wars, pestilence, cruelty, or oppression or accepted the Spencerian premise that the state should assume no responsibility for education. Yet, evolutionary thought clearly shaped educators' conceptions of society and the individual, of man's limited capacity to implement change, and, hence, of the restricted social function of the school.[4]

Although Spencerian influences usually remained implicit in educators' rhetoric, periods of national crisis such as the Great Strikes of 1877 or the Panic of 1893 prompted more explicit and dogmatic pronouncements. It then became apparent not only that educators accepted the Spencerian concept of division of labor but also that most subscribed as well to its social corollary, a rigidly defined class system which education had little capacity to modify except by developing character and inculcating morality. As socioeconomic problems of industrialization and urbanization intensified, educators became more explicit in their application of Spencerian social tenets to interpretrations of crises. James C. Boykin, the U.S. Bureau of Education specialist on urban schools, for example, did not hesitate to ascribe social and economic dislocations to failures of character among "the paupers, . . . the thriftless, [and] . . . the depraved" who congregated in cities. Nicholas Murray Butler similarly warned of dangers emanating from an ignorant and amoral urban proletariat.[5]

Despite such explicit statements, however, it is the tone rather than the substance of educational rhetoric that supports the conclusion that Darwinist precepts of struggle, selection, and survival of the fittest were significant facets of educators' thought. Virtually every major article, address, or essay concerned with the educational problems of the city in the late 1800s reveals their influence. Indeed, by the turn of the century the impact of various versions of evolutionary philosophy —and of the thought of Andrew Carnegie and Horatio Alger —had become clearly evident. Identification of sources of urban problems, in schools or out, focused increasingly upon the failures of individual character rather than upon the disjunctions emanating from the urban-industrial milieu. Similarly, remedies proposed for urban educational problems concentrated upon inculcating the values of self-sacrifice, duty, morality, patriotism, industry, and thrift rather than upon attacking the specific dislocations underlying slums, poverty, underemployment, and crime in cities.[6]

Not all Gilded Age educators owed their intellectual debts to Spencer, Carnegie, or Alger, however; William Torrey Harris, Superintendent of St. Louis schools (1860–1880) and U.S. Commissioner of Education (1889–1906), is one of the best and most influential examples of those who did not. Yet Harris, too, understood society in evolutionist terms and the school's role in it as a limited one. Although he explicitly rejected the determinism of Spencer's *Social Statics,* Harris did subscribe to what Merle Curti has called a "right-wing [non-Marxian] Hegelianism" which "satisfied religious and idealistic aspirations, paid tribute to the cult of individualism and self-help, and . . . subordinated the mass of individuals to existing institutions." Because he was thus committed, he saw little value in curricular innovation that departed from the formal "branches" or disciplines—grammar, literature and art, mathematics, history and geography, and language—which he regarded as the "five windows of the soul." Harris, whom Beatrice Webb described as an "excellent elderly gentleman—essentially an 'elementary' or 'Sunday school' teacher type—with a taste for writing fluffy pamphlets on 'social evolution,'" adhered to the doctrine that the successful, or "fit," had an obligation, though a limited one, to assist the disadvantaged in uplifting themselves and that it was indeed possible for any member of society to "teach himself to be a capitalist." The best education, through traditional methods, produced citizens committed to the established order, aware of their place in it, and respectful of the institution of property.[7]

Furthermore, Harris asserted, the "characteristic instruments of modern civilization are the railroad, the daily newspaper, and the common school," and he firmly believed that the function of the school involved the instruction of the masses in the uses of the railroad and the newspaper in order to attain a higher level of civilization. Harris, always the optimist, sincerely believed that achievement possible through existing educational institutions and practices for all but those whose characters contained serious flaws. Success, however, he predicated upon the character of the individual and his willingness to capitalize, in every ethical way, upon the opportunities traditional education offered. Thus, Harris's intellectual position, though derived from different sources, led to conclusions that varied little from those of his contemporaries and colleagues.[8]

Such conceptions of the school, the individual, and society, regardless of philosophical origins, could prompt few radical innovations in education to mitigate urgent social dislocations. That they should comprise a major facet of the educational creed is not surprising, however. Variations of social evolutionist thought suffused the intellectual atmosphere of the Gilded Age, influencing even Francis Wayland Parker, hailed as a leader in the democratization of the school, who defined the role of education as molding character in order to eradicate the "terrible evils of shiftlessness, carelessness, and incomplete work." Although Parker recognized that the character of members of all classes might require equal attention, his identification of the sources of social dislocations resembled that of his more conservative colleagues. A recent educational historian has explained the pervasiveness of the social aspects of evolutionist thought in terms of its coincidence with demands for schools that not only identified the fit but also provided for their survival.[9] More important, however, is the simpler consideration that Spencerian doctrines apparently coincided with the facts of Gilded Age social and economic life, at least as they were interpreted by educational decision makers.

Nevertheless, acceptance of the social precepts of evolutionary thought left educators, who never renounced their basic commitment to traditional American ideals, in the paradoxical and uncomfortable position of assenting to social stratification while preaching social harmony, mobility, equality, and democracy. Nor was the contradiction ever resolved, except by subtly redefining the concept of democracy through political reorganization. By retaining the processes of popular suffrage while transferring to the "better elements" of society authority to designate options—either measures or men—among which voters might choose, reformers achieved a compromise of sorts. This issue seems to vindicate Hays's analysis of the discrepancy between educator's reform ideology and practice. However, educators were actually more confused than deceptive—and perhaps, in reality, only self-deceptive.

In the closing decades of the century, it became apparent that educators defined the public school—and sincerely accepted the definition—as an agency for maintaining harmonious relationships among social classes rather than for changing relationships or eliminating barriers, an agency for creating "homogeneous American citizens" as well as "intelligent voters, fair-minded jurymen, upright judges, discreet and honest legislators, and incorruptible executive officers."[10] More significantly, educators became increasingly willing to define the nature of such virtues for the masses, particularly for the less easily homogenized—the urban poor, and more specifically, the immigrant urban poor.

Although the Americanization movement in public education is most commonly associated with the period between the world wars, educators in late nineteenth-century cities had already defined the necessity, not only to adjust the alien to life—especially urban life—in America, but also to control the foreigner and neutralize his presumed threat to native values. Fear, perhaps, is too extreme a term to apply to reformers' attitudes toward immigrants; yet despite obvious feelings of intellectual, moral, and often ethnic superiority, educators revealed a persistent apprehensiveness about the newcomers. Expressions of anxiety that Irish elements plotted to control schools in order to spread popish notions, that the very presence of eastern Europeans and Asians corrupted American children, that various aliens sought to use ward school offices as springboards to higher and more lucrative positions, and that immigrant workers displaced native craftsmen all support the conclusion that educators were more specifically concerned with the impact of ethnic groups upon the public school and American life than with the school's influence upon the immigrant. Thus, when attention focused upon the immigrant, it most frequently concerned such matters as social control, teaching English, improving attendance, raising hygienic standards within the school, and inculcating the educators' own value systems.[11] Only rarely did immigrant homes or cultures elicit genuine concern.

Indeed, by 1900, urban educators had begun to take obvious pride in their accomplishments in detaching immigrant children from their native heritage. For example, New York City District Superintendent Julia Richman wrote in 1905:

My heart beats faster and my eyes grow moist when I hear it. These children, refugees from Russia and Roumania, with hate in their hearts for the land of their birth, turn loving eyes to the flag of the land of their adoption, and there is genuine fervor in their pledge [of allegiance].

Another reformer expressed equally undisguised delight that a foreign child would soon "begin to be ashamed of her beautiful Spanish name, and will revise its spelling in deference to [her] friends' linguistic limitations."[12] Few educators or reformers inquired whether the land of the immigrants' adoption had in return adopted the immigrants; for most, such superficialities as saluting the flag with fervor, learning the language, acquiring regular habits, or anglicizing a name seem to have constituted sufficient and successful Americanization.

For others, however, including the eminent educationist Professor Ellwood P. Cubberly of Stanford University, the process involved much more, including the school's active effort to implement the tasks of breaking

up these [immigrant] groups or settlements, to assimilate and amalgamate these people as part of our American race, and to implant in their children, so far as can be done, the Anglo-Saxon conception of righteousness, law and order, and popular government, and to awaken in them a reverence for our national life which we as a people hold to be of abiding worth.[13]

Significantly, Cubberly neglected the social or economic problems of the immigrant himself, the contribution the newcomer might make to American life, the specific role the urban school might play in his adaptation to American society, and most obviously, the fact that in the immigrant culture itself there might indeed be something of "abiding worth."

Most educators shared Cubberly's limited vision of the urban immigrant's social, cultural, and economic life. And they were even more apprehensive of his political potential. For not only did aliens presumably lack experience in democracy, they also frequently were carriers of radicalism or anarchism. Moreover, their concentration in cities furnished a potential "army" for demagogues who could capitalize upon their ignorance, poverty, and lack of experience in order to seize domestic political institutions, including urban school systems. That political education to avert such a calamity constituted a basic responsibility of the school was hardly debatable. But just as clearly, the dangerous element was the adult and not the child, making the creation of a responsible electorate at best a long-range proposition. The most obvious and effective alternative involved circumscription of politicians and their supposedly ignorant supporters to insure that only the best men, among whom educators clearly numbered themselves, managed the affairs of cities and schools. As has already been seen, educators moved, often in concert with municipal reform movements, to do precisely that. Ironically, to accomplish their ends and control masses of politically untutored voters, urban educational reformers and their lay allies frequently adopted the strategy and tactics of their opponents—and created an urban political machine.[14]

To be sure, a few educational leaders turned to immigration restriction to solve political problems, but most remained committed to the strategy of limiting choices, convinced that progress itself ultimately would provide solutions for social, economic, and political dislocations. Indeed, faith in Progress —often derived from evolutionist thought—and in education as its instrument remained a central tenet of educational orthodoxy in the Gilded Age.

However, schoolmen of that era were "progressives" in neither the political nor the educational sense in which the term has come to be used, despite their institutional tinkering with the structures of urban school systems. For to be a progressive implied acceptance of man's dynamic role in the initiation and guidance of social change, and this most urban educational leaders were unprepared to do. Their faith in progress emanated from two sources, neither of which implied radical social change and both of which tended to vitiate urban school reform. One is found in the traditional

American faith—dating from Franklin, Jefferson, and Mann —in the pragmatic value of education itself as an effective instrument for the integration of the masses of citizens into the civic, economic, and cultural life of the Republic. Although dissenters from the simplistic interpretation of that tradition, including Dewey and his followers, recognized that what was taught and how it was taught were more significant than the mere exposure of children to the rudiments of traditional pedagogy, the bulk of the educational literature of the era exudes confidence in just such externals. Indeed, even Francis Wayland Parker, whom Dewey called the father of progressive education, found it possible to ignore the findings of social reformers and insist that "the log school-house, the old weatherbeaten structure, has evolved into beautiful, well ventilated, well warmed and well furnished temples of learning."[15]

Because more children attended increasing numbers of more efficiently managed schools, the assumption that education was accomplishing its purpose and that, given sufficient time, all would be well apparently prevailed. Even more important in precluding significant educational reform, however, was a Pollyanna syndrome common among educators. Joseph M. Rice, for example, found that even in cities where the worst conditions existed, principals and superintendents radiated pride in the accomplishments of their schools. The remark of a Baltimore administrator summarized the attitude of many of his colleagues: "If things are perfect or nearly so, why interfere?"[16] Such sentiments could hardly motivate effective urban educational reform.

Nor could the second source of educators' faith in progress: the milieu of the Gilded Age. In conjunction with the evolutionist nature of their thought, conditions confirmed the conviction that few modifications beyond reorganization and expansion were needed to make education a vehicle for spectacular civic, economic, and cultural achievement. For whatever else it was, the Gilded Age was a dynamic era, one that witnessed astounding advancements in science, technology, industry, medicine, and nearly all other fields of human endeavor. Educators, like many of their contemporaries, responded positively to their environment and interpreted events as evidence of unswerving Progress. Although the theologically tempered Comtean positivism of William Torrey Harris provides an explicit example of educators' confidence and of the affinity between their thought and Andrew Carnegie's triumphant democracy,[17] the attitudes of others are less easily documented. Nevertheless, the tenor of thirty years of educational literature including the yearly *NEA Proceedings,* publications of the U.S. Bureau of Education, and the wealth of articles appearing in contemporary lay and professional journals makes the dominant attitude of educators, particularly that of highly articulate and prolific urban administrators, evident. To be sure, confidence in the promise of urban-industrial society was less than universal. However, the educational profession produced no Henry Adams.

On the contrary, educators seemed to discern improvement in all aspects of the human condition. Despite concern for the foreign-born and the politically ignorant, and for the waning of traditional ideals and values, few educators were confirmed pessimists. Even the city, in some ways threatening, embodied potential for Progress. Furthermore, developments in science and technology promised direct and indirect benefits for education, hence, for humanity. Psychology, applied to education through child study, and Bertillon's system of anatomical measurements could help school men detect personality traits, educational potential, and otherwise hidden characteristics and tendencies. Less directly, scientific and technological advances offered a better life to all and greater leisure for education and culture. Indeed, confidence allowed many educators to ignore the painful realities which often accompanied the Progress they lauded and led them to agree with Cubberly that

An increasing proportion of our population have been freed from the mere drudgery of life and have been permitted to devote themselves to the work of extending culture and advancing the art and science of the race.[18]

Although essentially accurate, Cubberly's assessment nevertheless implies several questions which he and his contemporaries failed to answer—in many cases even failed to ask. Who,
for example, made up the increasing proportion freed from
drudgery? Did technological progress also entail an inverse
reaction, reducing some others to drudgery? What was the
school's responsibility, if any, to those who were not benefiting
from extended culture and advancing science?

If faith in Progress mitigated educators' tensions concerning social change and permitted them to evade questions concerning the less gratifying aspects of urban-industrial society,
so too did their own self-evaluation. For strains of elitism
and paternalism permeated urban educational reform as they
did similar movements of the Gilded Age. Elitism, however,
should not be construed as a manifestaton of a sense of
"displacement" or evidence of "status anxiety" among educators. Nor does evidence support the conclusion that educators
resented the rise of the new industrial and commercial classes;
on the contrary, they tended to identify with those newly
emergent elements of society.[19] Only in the realm of politics
and professionalism did educators express sentiments that
might be interpreted as status anxiety, and they moved reso-
lutely to alleviate both of those problems through structural
reorganization of city school systems and the subsequent en-
trenchment of their positions. The educators' elitism emerged
as a firm conviction—supported by evolutionist and Anglo-
Saxon thought—of intellectual and moral superiority accompanied by an intense, almost missionary, sense of duty and a
pervasive willingness to exercise their obligation by dictating
standards of political, social, and economic morality. Although
the sense of intellectual and moral ascendancy revealed itself
in numerous subtle ways, it is most clearly apparent in attitudes and actions involved in efforts to reform urban school
structure and to redefine the role of the school in urban-
industrial society, activities in which educators revealed their
kinship with contemporary municipal and social reformers.

In his study of the era's liberal reformers, John G. Sproat

observed, "In the last analysis, good government meant government responsive to the demands of those who clamored for it." With but little modification, the same assessment applies to educational reform. For the definition of good education embodied educators' own conceptions of what it should be, in both structure and function. And in both cases, definitions emanated from elitist presumptions about themselves and the remainder of society. Educational reformers of the Gilded Age demonstrated an aversion to partisan politics in municipal affairs, an animosity shared with other reformers of the same period. At the heart of the sentiments of both groups lay contempt for those involved in urban politics: machines and bosses, ward heelers, and masses of ignorant voters. Moreover, to both groups the apparent basis of city politics in the crassest sort of materialism constituted a flagrant contradiction to their own ethical standards, a condition emphasized by the participation of the "dangerous classes."[20].

Logic and a sense of superiority dictated the remedies: eliminate untrustworthy elements and erect city school systems that deposited and maintained control in the hands of the reliable elements of the community. For educators knew, "a system is practically good or bad according as it tends to bring *the right kind of men* into public service and keep them there," and they were unwilling to leave the attraction, selection, or retention of those men to chance or to traditional political processes. Instead, civil service would assure a higher degree of professionalism among teachers and administrators while eliminating political influence. Logic also prescribed elimination of those elements upon whom political trimmers relied for access to power, namely, the ignorant voters, and this meant restructuring school systems to ensure election of school board members from the city at large rather than from the wards. Thus, the local school committee would no longer provide an easily accessible apprenticeship for politicians, the greasy mechanic and saloon-keeper would be eliminated from competition, and natural selection would allow choices from among those obviously best suited for office: "lawyers and businessmen who handle large enterprises." Indeed, some educators would have eliminated a popular participation entirely and made all school positions entirely appointive, assuming that men of property—equated with stability—would be chosen.[21]

Thus, educators made their self-conceptions abundantly clear, not only in the school problems they identified but also in the remedies they prescribed. Typically, the upper-echelon urban educator visualized himself as an expert, one who understood not only the moral, economic, and professional dangers of political involvement in public schools but also the most effective means to avert those dangers. It is tempting to ascribe efforts to centralize authority and retain it in their own hands as a quest for power, but to draw such a conclusion would be to oversimplify. For the consistency of educators' thought and action makes it apparent that they felt, along with their consciousness of moral and intellectual superiority, a sense of ethical ascendancy and an obligation to disseminate and perpetuate the values of which they presumed they were the custodians. While these motivations reveal themselves in both the rhetoric and practice of city school reform, they are even more distinct in efforts to define the nature and purpose of education itself.

For educational leaders, as well as for many other reformers, there was no problem—political, economic, or social—so difficult or so complex "that stern morality would not solve it." Nor did educators apply their versions of morality to the public school timidly. Many, like William Torrey Harris, insisted that inferior beings existed to provide opportunity for the superior to fulfill their mission in life. And typically, educators presumed that their mission involved providing moral leadership and instruction for the masses. Equally typical was their assumption that such people had no moral leaders or standards of their own. Moreover, urban educational leaders premised the standards they sought to impose less upon analyses of the socioeconomic realities of urban life than upon presumptions concerning morality and the nature of education. Unlike settlement workers, they made few forays into the lower wards of their cities and therefore blindly defined the primary task of the school as rectifying "inherited vicious propensities" which they assumed existed among the "class of children" who would soon become members of the working —and voting—classes. The morality educators sought to instill remained founded upon individual virtues, and stressed temperance, social purity, industry, thrift, and manners rather than the social necessities of life in urban society. In the slums of New York City, a school that taught neat handwriting, erect posture, alert attention, and good manners "did its job," and one in Philadelphia that taught similar virtues and produced immigrant children who read "with a cultivated inflection" received similar praise. Even the sciences became didactic; a plea, for example, to add astronomy to the *primary* curriculum emphasized its moral and disciplinary value.[22]

Indeed, even when educators did recognize the social nature of urban problems, remedies varied little in moralistic tone. To eliminate most city problems, social harmony based upon common morality became a major pedagogical goal. Should that fail, children of the "notorious criminal classes" should be separated from their parents and peers and sent to industrial schools—preferably in the country—to learn the proper virtues. Conditions of urban society admittedly provided sources of social dislocation, but educational responses remained rooted firmly in the soil of individual virtue. "To root up vice, to lessen crime, to lift up the people, . . . and to save the sacred principles of republicanism" was the school's central function, and "promptness, regularity, and silence" the primary virtues.[23]

The purpose here, it must be emphasized, is neither to denigrate the values urban educators proclaimed nor even to evaluate their relevance as solutions for problems of urban underemployment, anomie, criminality, vice, or political corruption. What is significant is the common assumption among educators that the problems resulted from the absence of such virtues among the urban masses and that local leadership lacked both ethical standards and capacity. To be sure, corruption did prevail in American cities of the time, but it was neither limited to, nor universal among, the masses whom educators found so lacking in virtue. Nevertheless—prompted by a sense of superiority, their missionary inclinations, and their growing detachment from the realities of urban life—educators dogmatically prescribed both political and ethical solutions for those same urban masses.

Educators in the Gilded Age clearly presumed that "they spoke *for* the nation rather than *to* it," and that their thought embodied the best principles of republican virtue. These attitudes—coupled with a congeries of ideas including evolutionist thought, a supreme faith in Progress, and a strong tendency toward elitism and paternalism—permitted them to overlook some of the contradictions in their ideology, which become apparent from the perspective of history. They could, for example, both assert that discontent provided the catalyst for Progress and sincerely define the public school as an instrument for pacifying the laboring classes and rendering them content with their lot.[24] Or they could preach democracy while salting their rhetoric with terms revealing conceptions of a clearly defined and rigid class structure, without recognizing the apparent paradox.

Yet it would be unfair and indeed inaccurate to categorize educators as ignorant, blind, or purposely self-seeking. Like many other Americans of that time, the era in which they lived confused them. It was a period that finds its essential unity only in the historian's generalizations and one complicated by the fact of urbanization. Furthermore, educators were frequently detached from the urban masses they proposed to educate, often by the very bureaucratic structures they had created and increasingly by spatially fragmented patterns of urban growth. Moreover, in common with others of their era, educators looked at once to the future and to the past: to the future and Progress for the improvements they so optimistically expected, and to the past—and often the rural-agrarian past—for the values they attempted to instill in the new urban-industrial society. Indeed, so pervasive was the commitment to the mystique of the rural-agrarian past that educators would not have challenged municipal reformer Frederic C. Howe who argued that "Human life seems to require a ground wire to the sod, a connection with Mother Earth to maintain its virility."[25] For many educators and laymen the school supplied that connection, and the influence of the pastoral tradition permeated many educational programs which had been designed explicitly to alleviate problems of urban-industrial society.

6

The Lure of the Country in Urban Education

It is better to be a country boy . . . than to be a nursling of a palace in the great city.
—John Lancaster Spalding

In 1933 Arthur M. Schlesinger, Sr., identified the "lure of the city" as a significant characteristic of late nineteenth-century American thought. The city functioned as a centripetal force attracting thousands of migrants to greater economic opportunities, broader social horizons, advanced cultural development, and other positive features commonly associated with urban life. Simultaneously, the countryside itself exerted a centrifugal force as a result of contrasting negative features of rural life: depressed conditions, isolation, and monotony.[1]

It is difficult to fault the essential accuracy of that analysis. Yet "lure of the country" also constituted a major intellectual trend which, in varied ways, influenced attempts to come to terms with emergent urban-industrial society. Attraction to rural-agrarion life styles has been persistent in American attitudes, but in the closing decades of the nineteenth century urbanization and industrialization seemed to challenge the pastoral dream and to demand its vigorous defense. To that task rallied intellectuals, writers, orators, and politicians— particularly those who saw only the penumbra of their own rural experience through a haze of nostalgia and who considered industrial society, and cities in particular, threatening to republican virtue, virility, and purity. The sentiments and ambivalences involved are perhaps best summarized in a remark by Henry S. Canby who experienced the transition in American society: "[W]e were town dwellers moved by instinct and tradition alike to reach back toward the farm."[2] Among those persuaded by such instincts and traditions, and marching in the vanguard of the defenders of the pastoral faith, were many of the nation's upper-echelon urban educators.

Some Americans, like Frederic C. Howe, envisioned the city as the nation's salvation, the setting in which "the ready responsiveness of democracy, under the close association which the city involves, forecasts a movement for the improvement of human society more hopeful than anything the world has known." However, such optimism, rare among Americans, was rarer still among American educators. To be sure, there was William Torrey Harris, who saw great potential in the city. The most prolific and articulate educational spokesman of his age, Harris was as optimistic as Howe, convinced that "the people in cities have the advantage of the world's discoveries in science, art, literature and history." Cities offered "to each of [their] inhabitants the inestimable blessings of society with the wise and the good," and for Harris the city represented a vast classroom which would "dissolve clanship and cultivate in its place independence of opinion and action."[3] Such opinions reflected not only Harris' positivism but also the optimism of his age. Still, though he most frequently spoke for a majority of his colleagues, the Commissioner's attitude toward cities was clearly a minority sentiment among educators.

Indeed, most American educators were hostile or, at best, ambivalent toward the city, and their sentiments coincided closely with those of Superintendent Lawton B. Evans of Augusta, Georgia. In response to a fellow administrator attending the NEA Convention of 1896, Evans asserted:

It is the nature of people to collect in communities. Man is the most gregarious of animals. His social instincts and capacities impel him to build cities and enjoy living in them. . . . It is true that cities are the centers of highest civilization, . . . [but] cities are also the centers of the greatest iniquity. The worthless, the idle, the wicked gravitate toward large centers. The force of cities is centripetal and attracts everything, good and bad alike.

Cities, Evans continued, were not in the best American tradition, for they did not stimulate individualism of the sort exemplified by "the strong and independent men of our nation." The truly great had been "born and bred in village and rural homes, away from the turmoil of city life, in quiet communion with nature in her grand an ennobling forms."[4] Evans' remarks indicate awareness of urbanization in American society. But they also reveal that, like many of his contemporaries, he felt less than optimistic concerning the change. There were, to be sure, admirable qualities in cities and in industrial society as well as the potential for progress not only in education but also in the general level of civilization. These, however, were concessions made grudgingly. Simultaneously, Evans articulated anxiety about the new environment's impact upon traditional ideals and values, nostalgia for a simpler past, and outright hostility toward the implications of urbanism.

The ideas of few Gilded Age educators deviated substantially from those of the Augusta superintendent. Although some could admit that "the city [school] affords superior training," even they qualified the concession with the assertion that "the country school produces the superior product." In fact, many educators shared the blatant antiurbanism of Roman Catholic Bishop John Lancaster Spalding of Peoria. A leader in both parochial and secular education, Spalding avowed:

At all events, that little school house, hardly bigger than a dry-goods box, above which no bough waves, around which no flowers bloom, near which no brook flows, is as it stands there by the dusty or muddy road, in solitude and nakedness, weather-beaten and discolored, a better place for education than one of our great factory-like structures. *It is in the country; and it is better . . . to be a country boy* than to be a nursling of a palace in a great city.[5]

Austere as it might be, the rural school was infinitely superior, simply because it was located in the country.

This was no isolated sentiment among educators. G. Stanley Hall, President of Clark University and leading exponent of child psychology, declared in rhetoric less colorful but no less emphatic than Spalding's that a sandpile offered greater educational potential than formalized school experience in the city. Similarly, Principal Francis Wayland Parker of Cook County Normal School vowed that educational opportunity was greater on a good farm than anywhere else on earth. The rural setting was simpler and more secure, and the farm child had incessant opportunity to use his eyes and his hands, to learn by doing, and to profit from activity and experience. For innumerable reasons, the rural child's prospects for happiness seemed far superior to those of his less fortunate urban counterpart, despite material advantages the city school might offer.[6]

The attitudes of Evans, Spalding, Hall, and Parker typified those of the majority of their profession, and the necessity to restore the fundamental contact between man and nature became one of the central elements in the pedagogical dialogue of the era. Schoolmen defined a principal problem facing the city teacher as the "impossibility of bringing [pupils] into genuine contact" with nature. There was something sinister—almost subversive and foreboding—in the cleavage cities created between man and his proper primary environment. To counter this, G. Stanley Hall admonished teachers to love nature and to "infect the children with it," and naturalist President David Starr Jordan of Stanford University evaluated as best those teachers who brought their charges closest to nature.[7] Educators were convinced not only that nature had something to say to man, but also that the message was dissipated in the urban setting which deprived city dwellers of the intellectual, psychological, moral, and physical benefits derived from intimate and immediate contact with his universe.

So potent was the commitment to the pastoral tradition and to the beneficence of nature that for at least one urban educator the solution to city school problems involved bringing the country school to the city. Preston Willis Search, Superintendent of Los Angeles Schools in 1895, insisted that urban schools ought to be replicas of those in the countryside, complete with ungraded classes, animals, and farmlike surroundings. The setting would revitalize the city child, develop his individualism, broaden his experience, and promote his moral, mental, and physical well-being, just as the rural experience had presumably done. Search believed that

The losses from reversion from the rural life to that of the city would be partially overcome. The farm, with its many lessons from Nature and its many trades and occupations possible, would be rich in instructive exercises. The gardens would bring back the forgotten touch with the soil, and the delights of animal life would awaken new human interest.[8]

Search did not specify just which new interests would be stimulated, but he was obviously certain that combining traditional education with occupational training and locating both in a quasi-rural setting in the city would remedy the ills of urban society. Although not all educators accepted the specifics of Search's solution or shared his sweeping optimism, many indeed concurred at least with the principles of his program and, to some degree, shared his near mysticism concerning the educational superiority of nature and the rural-agrarian environment.

It is not surprising, however, that they should. As Roderick Nash has suggested, Americans at the turn of the century felt acute anxiety concerning changes overtaking them, and not the least threatening of those changes were the inroads urbanization was making into their pristine wilderness. Both the historian Frederick Jackson Turner and the census returns had confirmed the closing of the frontier, and educators and laymen alike voiced their concern that the city was permanently severing man's "ground wire to the sod." Americans felt that they were "the last inheritors of that intuitive faith in nature which had made Wordsworth a poet and Emerson a philosopher."[9] Earlier in the century, reformers like Charles Loring Brace of the New York City Children's

Aid Society responded by sending thousands of city children on excursions to the countryside or by placing them in rural foster homes. And others, including Frederick Law Olmsted and his followers, sought solutions in the creation of natural enclaves within urban boundaries, refuges where city dwellers might experience the influences of a transplanted nature. Educators revealed their own anxieties both explicitly and implicitly in programs appended to the urban common school curriculum: nature study, school gardens, vacation schools, and manual training.

The "nature study idea," as it was originally called, emerged in the last quarter of the century to become the more formal branch of study, natural science. By either name, however, it was an all-encompassing program, so comprehensive that Nicholas Murray Butler could describe it as a discipline touching "the universe at many more points than one; and properly interpreted, . . . classed among the humanities as truly as the study of language itself." Deriving impetus from men like Butler, David Starr Jordan, and agricultural education champion Liberty Hyde Bailey of Cornell University, traditional interest in nature and concern for a changing environment merged to create an educational movement that encouraged the study of nature as a vehicle for physical, social, and moral regeneration. Because its conception was broad, nature study could take diverse forms. For some, it involved a paradoxical synthesis of nostalgia with a very modern faith in science and emerged as an energetic drive to add the new discipline, natural science, to the common school curriculum.[10]

Other educators subscribed to a more romantic or mystic view, typified by the assertion of California Superintendent of Public Instruction Ira G. Hoitt that "trees everywhere exert a moral influence; . . . that fact we know and feel in our every day's experience." Nature and her works should be the principal teachers, and for many educators school gardens constituted the favored means to facilitate the operation for urban school children. By allotting small schoolyard plots to city students and encouraging them to become miniature yeo-men in the Jeffersonian tradition, school-garden advocates hoped to promote curiosity; instill industriousness, skill, and self-reliance; teach order, cleanliness, and punctuality; excite esthetic sensitivity; and prevent moral degeneration. Contact with the soil would stimulate "public spirit in the children . . . [and] the regard for manual labor." In short, faith in nature's influence made school gardens seem panaceas for the apparent shortcomings of urban-industrial society; they would be new "pioneers of civilization, promoters of practical progress, and sources of prosperity in communities." Even the usually devastating critic Joseph M. Rice acclaimed Cook County Normal School for making the garden and nature-park ideas central to its teacher-training program.[11] For Americans anxious about the implications of a changing society, school gardens and nature study in the regular curriculum seemed to promise at least a tentative link with a long-cherished but disappearing pastoral tradition.

Moreover, it seemed not only feasible but also beneficial to extend the potential beyond the regular school year and thereby expand their impact. Summer vacation schools were initially the province of private charity. However, professional educators' commitment to nature as teacher soon brought the program under the auspices of public school systems in large- and medium-sized cities. An ideology perhaps more perceptive than that of nature-study or school-garden proponents impelled vacation-school advocates. For they explicitly recognized needs among urban children for recreational and social activities and facilities other than those furnished by city streets. Nevertheless, a pervasive and tenacious commitment to the rural-agrarian tradition also remained an integral part of the vacation-school concept. It sought, for example, programs capable of

supplying the children with something that would take the place of those old duties of childhood that had disappeared, of furnishing manual activities and problems similar to those with which our ancestors had to deal, and restoring to the child something of the environment of nature which he had lost [in the city].

Indeed, the vacation school frequently fused aspects of the nature-study and school-garden ideas with more traditional moralistic aims. In New York City, for example, young agrarians worked individual four-by-twelve-foot "farms" in DeWitt Clinton Park. And Chicago made nature study the central feature of its vacation-school program.[12]

Despite educators' faith in nature and the vigor of their efforts to restore elements of the natural experience to urban children, neither nature study, school gardens, nor vacation schools produced significant results. They did not alleviate the problems of the urban environment; nor did they substantially augment the children's ability to cope with them, for apparent reasons. Lay critics charged that most of the real benefits of nature suffered dilution when its study became a formal discipline: "when educators . . . herded natural history into the curriculum, they barred out the worship and made nature into just another commodity." Educators, too, found that nature fell far short of their expectations as a pedagogical tool. Obviously, they had expected more than they should and ignored the minimal relevance of the concepts taught to the realities of urban life. In any case, numerous cities reported that with rare exceptions natural history experiments had failed.[13] So also had school gardens and vacation schools.

Yet there is little evidence that failure diminished faith in nature or commitment to the values of the rural-agrarian past. Nor did educators ponder seriously the reasons for the failure. G. Stanley Hall, for example, deplored the persistent use of agrarian imagery in school books and intelligence tests for urban children but continued to insist that "the material of the city is no doubt inferior in pedagogic value to the country experience." Hall's comment reveals an intellectual dichotomy he and many of his colleagues shared with their fellow citizens in the Gilded Age, a durable habit of thought which inhibited efforts to make the school an institution rele-

vant to urban-industrial society. Henry S. Canby later re-
called the effect of the dualism upon students in Wilmington,
Delaware; the ethics taught "were agrarian ethics, and we
town dwellers already felt their frequent inapplicability and,
without realizing the cause, wearied of similes drawn entirely
from agriculture."[14] Apparently, educators were less sensitive
to the contradiction than were their students.

Indeed, agrarian similes—or at least undertones of the
rural-agrarian past—permeated even the one major educational movement of the Gilded Age that should have been an
explicit response to the demands of urban-industrial society—
the drive to add manual training to the common school curriculum.

Clearly, educators recognized the socioeconomic implications of urbanization and industrialization, but they related
them to the school only reluctantly. In 1876, for example,
Commissioner John Eaton noted the continuing impact of the
economic crisis of 1873 upon education. Conditions demanded rigid retrenchment in public schools, the result of
impaired relations between capital and labor and stiffening
resistance to taxation for school purposes. But he also reported continuing progress and even reason for self-congratu-
lation, for the nation's first century had "closed unmarred by
those bloody conflicts between representatives of capital and
labor" which accompanied industrialization elsewhere, and
he credited the good fortune to the influence of the common
school. A year later, following the Great Strikes of 1877,
Eaton's confidence had been abated, but by no means ex-
tinguished, when he wrote that

the lesson taught by these outbreaks has apparently in some
cases stopped short of tracing them to their source in individual
character, and has failed to discover the part to be performed
by education as a means of protection against their recurrence.

Labor unrest had resulted from the "systematic vagrancy of
the ignorant, vicious, and criminal classes," and the commissioner warned capital to "weigh the cost of the mob and
the tramp against the expense of universal and sufficient edu-

cation." He assumed that failures of character, not rapidly changing economic conditions, had produced disturbances and articulated faith in the efficacy of education to insure against further dislocations without major departure from traditional practices. Instead of change, conditions demanded more extensive dissemination of standard education to build character resistant to the instigators of such outbursts as the Great Strikes.[15]

Although most of Eaton's professional contemporaries shared his views, not all accepted traditional curricula as adequate to the exigencies of urban-industrial society. Perhaps the largest group of dissenters were the disciples of manual training who, though accepting the fundamental tenets of traditional education, initiated the most persistent nineteenth-century effort to modify the content of American public education. The concept of training for work has an extensive history in American education, but the nexus formed by coincidental industrialization and urbanization precipitated a revival of the idea and the formalization of its doctrines. However, Russian displays at the Philadelphia Centennial Exposition of 1876 provided the specific stimulus: exhibits from the Moscow Imperial Technical School which, under the direction of Victor Della Vos, had developed revolutionary techniques in tool-work instruction. Della Vos's system isolated the basic processes of the shop and concentrated upon instruction rather than production. Models illustrating the method inspired American educators, who mobilized to alleviate problems of their society by revising traditional common school curricula to include instruction in tool work and drawing.[16]

Manual training rapidly gained the momentum necessary to become a major educational reform movement of the Gilded Age. Its major spokesman, President Calvin M. Woodward of Washington University in St. Louis, enunciated its goals and purposes. Manual training would supplement traditional curriculum and make it more relevant to urban-industrial society. Specifically, innovation would keep students in school longer, mold moral and intellectual character, facilitate sounder occupational choices, assure greater spiritual and material success, and elevate the status of the manual trades. Woodward, whose goal was to "put the whole boy to school," expected industrial education to reduce unemployment by teaching skills and to alleviate absenteeism by stimulating interest. As his initial experiment at the St. Louis Manual Training School gained publicity, the movement's supporters increased and advanced more and more arguments in its favor, prompting cities across the nation to experiment with the program. Indeed, within a decade and a half of its inception, manual training had become an accepted part of common school curricula. By 1892, educators no longer questioned the pedagogical validity of manual training but only its economic and physical feasibility.[17]

Moreover, as acceptance grew, manual training also acquired a broader conceptual scope, becoming a virtual panacea for society's dislocations. One advocate saw in it the Pestalozzian concept of "equal cultivation of the head, the heart and the hand"; another considered it a means to develop esthetic values and "mind culture"; and still others felt that manual training would provide a bulwark against materialism, give children practical experiences, keep them off the labor market, and "get back the heart and sinew of man to giant oaks once more." One even envisioned a generation of blacksmith-philosophers in the mold of Elihu Burritt emerging from school workshops. Goals and expectations were high indeed and reflected the traditional aims and general optimism of American education, including indoctrination of potential workers with the Spencerian dictum of the right of the fittest to survive and progress. Manual training, however, also romanticized labor as the natural condition of man and insisted that, in fact, no difference existed between the activity and the condition of the man who stoked the furnace and the one who owned the steel mill. Both should acknowledge their reciprocal duties and the joys of work. The feminine version of manual training, home economics, also revealed similar class conceptions and goals of social harmony in its objectives:

One of the vexing problems of today—the servant-girl question—will be less troublesome to the home-makers of the land . . . if the housewives have the ability . . . to do the tasks they set for the ignorant, untrained foreign girl who reigns in the kitchen.

In short, public schools might, through manual training, fulfill their obligations to instill moral standards, obliterate class conflict, build sound character, and—according to one advocate—even prevent divorce. Indeed, patriotism itself demanded its addition to the common school curriculum because

this morally industrial education is the only possible measure which can relieve us from the dangerous classes of criminals, from the threatening army of tramps, and from the convulsions, mobs, and anarchy which are coming upon us, when millions of unskilled and poorly educated workmen living near the precipice of famine are liable to be tumbled over its edge by any sudden tilting of the balance of trade, or the fluctuations of markets, even if the curse of monopoly and speculation were removed.

Despite such sensitivity to many of the prevailing problems of urban-industrial society, however, most manual training disciples deviated little from the goals and objectives of their more traditionalist critics.[18]

And criticism abounded, including objections to manual training's expedient and simplistic outlook, its materialism, its possible contribution to recurrent overproduction, its encouragement of early employment and expansion of the surplus labor pool, its "class legislation" characteristics, and its potential restriction upon the freedom of occupational choice. Some, including William Torrey Harris, contended that manual training objectives lacked realism, for only 3 percent of all workers at that time were employable in trades for which common schools could prepare them. Whether Harris's calculations were precisely accurate may be debated. Nevertheless, he did observe an important phenomenon which manual training advocates apparently chose to ignore, the fact of technological displacement. To be sure, the emerging factory system did increase demands for labor. But the skills needed were in technologically oriented categories such as tool making rather than the traditional crafts which manual training emphasized. Opponents of the program argued these points throughout the period; yet its disciples ignored technological displacement and industrial demands for increasing specialization, continuing to insist simply that "the invention of a new tool, a grand new labor-saving machine . . . adds new power and dignity to skilled hands."[19]

All of this, of course, raises the question: why were manual training advocates either unaware of the trend or ignoring it? One obvious explanation involves the relative rapidity with which society and its economic relationships changed; historical hindsight focuses trends and patterns to a greater precision than is possible for those who experience them. Moreover, intellectual currents influenced manual training supporters as they did other educators; the concepts of social Darwinism and Spencerian thought, positivism and the belief in Progress, the doctrines of laissez faire economics, and an Alger-like confidence permeate their rhetoric and literature. But most significant, they shared with other Americans a distinct and sincere, though often subconscious, preference for the ideals, values, and conditions of rural-agrarian America over those of urban-industrial society, and that attitude permeated their programs

For many, pastoralism remained only implicit in what they said and wrote. But others made their preferences explicit, arguing that "the little shop at the crossroads was far superior to the great factories of today where piece-work tends rather to stultify than to elevate those who are compelled to follow it." And the leading exponent of manual training in the public schools, President Francis Amasa Walker of Massachusetts Institute of Technology, understood the program not as an adaptation to industrial society but as a means to replace something lost in the urban setting:

In the country, the boy finds a hundred opportunities alike

at work and at play, for acquiring much of that which can only be given to the city boy by way of formal instruction. . . . [T]he country boy has incessant occasion to use his hands and his eyes; to observe, to plan, to do.

In the ideas of Calvin M. Woodward, nostalgia for the farm and the countryside was less apparent. Still, his social and economic goals were fused with moral values premised upon the craftsmanship ethic rather than upon the realities of the factory.[20]

Proponents of manual training shared attitudes with many other educators of the Gilded Age. Their models, however, were neither farms nor farmers. Instead, they were the "little shop at the crossroads," the blacksmith-philosopher Elihu Burritt, and men with the heart and sinew of giant oaks. They were right, of course, on at least one score: piecework in the factories—or in slum sweatshops—offered a less than elevating experience. Still, educators' commitment to re-creating the experiences of the village workshop in the city school could offer few realistic solutions to the problems of children in urban society. Like nature study, manual training programs were frequently tinged with a nostaliga that made them more relevant to the rural-agrarian past than to the urban-industrial present.

That educational leaders should yearn for a simpler past is not surprising. Most had developed their attitudes, if not on a farm, in a rural community, or small town, then at least in an atmosphere that esteemed and honored the Jeffersonian tradition. They had matured and been educated in a society that revered the pioneer spirit and rustic virtues, produced Emerson, Thoreau, Bryant, Parkman, Whitman, and William Jennings Bryan, and, in its innocence, rejected the supposedly effete urbanized civilization of Europe. To minds formed in such a tradition, the intrusion of the city and the factory into a previously unspoiled environment would be understandably distressing. Educators in the late 1800s exposed their distress in attitudes toward the city and in the nature of their efforts to respond to urban society. Meanwhile, they continued to long for the "small, unpainted schoolhouse in the remote country district." Perhaps they exhibited early symptoms of the "Marlboro-man" syndrome which permeates twentieth-century advertising, or perhaps they sincerely believed that contact with Nature—most frequently capitalized—produced an individual who was somehow finer morally, physically, and intellectually. Whatever their motivations, urbanization was to most educators a contradiction of their ethical and cultural traditions. "As the antipode of civilization, of cities, and of machines, wilderness [or farms or Nature] could be associated with the virtues these entities lacked."[21]

Despite a preference for the earlier environment, however, urban educators clearly understood that it no longer existed. They had been so informed not only by their colleagues and the census returns but also by developments they could scarcely ignore. Some, including educational psychologist Charles DeGarmo, even recognized the nature, permanence, and demands of urban society with some precision. Although he did not describe urbanization as a process, DeGarmo was conscious of its characteristics and its requirements when he wrote:

A city represents a system of reciprocal activities, duties, concessions, and benefits. Social co-operation in the city . . . is a necessity. . . . Yet even in these vast centers of population the ideals of a primitive community still prevail; for the dominant ideal . . . in this country is that of essentially non-social individualism.

DeGarmo also recognized that such individualism, combined with public apathy and educational traditionalism, prevented the sort of reform necessary to make the public school effective in an urban social environment.[22]

The city and industrial society demanded new ideals of community and cooperation and simultaneously provided the means for their attainment. But the educational understandings essential to make the city school an effective instrument for adjustment to novel conditions were not to be products of the Gilded Age. For educational leaders were too committed to the ideals and values of a past era to make it possible. Too many were satisfied to say with William H. Maxwell, "It is enough for us to know that in proportion to the increase in the urban population, insanity and crime increase."[23] It may have been true, but it was certainly not enough for educators to know. The fact is, however, that most educators' conceptions of urban society coincided closely with those of Maxwell, Evans, Spalding, and Hall rather than with those of men like DeGarmo. They were compelled by the "lure of the country," and inappropriate responses to the educational needs of the city frequently resulted—ironically at a time when John Dewey was attempting to make the school an agency for the restoration of the sense of community so often lost in the urban-industrial setting.

Although urban problems and the demise of traditional rural-agrarian society did not comprise the whole of the educational debate of the Gilded Age, it is clear that both drew more than passing attention. Those who articulated concern were not all luminaries in their profession. Yet their status was sufficiently substantial to permit them to speak to and for their colleagues and to influence the nature of urban educational programs. These leaders recognized many of the implications of urbanization, but they neither comprehended the process nor committed themselves to the city. Indeed, ambivalence—or even antagonism—most frequently characterized their attitudes. Consequently, responses to the city involved nostalgic efforts to restore elements of a past that perhaps never was. There is, to be sure, validity in the importance educators attached—and often continue to attach[24]—to nature and to the rural-agrarian tradition; in their recognition that positive elements of both were absent from the city there is value. And perhaps it was indeed "better to be a country boy" in Gilded Age America. However, the realities involved city children and their immediate experiences. For them, neither nature study nor miniature farms nor re-created village workshops provided adequate models or effective solutions to educational problems in an expanding urban society.

7

Compensatory Education:

Control Versus Reform

> *Better build schoolrooms for the boy*
> *Than cells and gibbets for the man.*
> —Eliza Cook

A new phrase, *compensatory education,* has become a commonplace in American educational rhetoric, and manifestations of its principles and implications are evident in local, state, and federal educational programs. The phrase—broadly defined and understood—refers to the concept that those denied the opportunity to attain normal levels of education can and should, through public action, be provided the means to do so. Implicit, also, is the understanding that those compensated will thus be able to assume their places as productive members of society. In current usage, compensatory education focuses generally, although not exclusively, upon members of urban ethnic minorities. Examples include local efforts to improve basic language skills of bilingual children, Head Start programs, the Educational Opportunity Program (EOP) in higher education, and the educative and retraining functions of the Office of Economic Opportunity (OEO), among others.[1]

Despite the recent coinage of the phrase and the rush to implement its principles, however, the basic concept of compensation is by no means new. Indeed, its precepts appear in ordinances in colonial Massachusetts, which enumerated penalties for failure to provide at least rudimentary education not only for children of freemen but also for those of indentured

115

servants. In the early years of the Republic, private charitable institutions, often partially supported by public funds, continued the tradition by providing basic schooling for the children of the poor. The same tradition also impelled the antebellum crusade for universal education through the common school and the Freedmen's Bureau and other efforts to educate former slaves after the Civil War. In the Gilded Age the tradition was manifest in the establishment of settlement kindergartens, the attempt to prepare children for a role in industrial society through manual training, and the effort to Americanize immigrant children through education.

The benevolence underlying such ventures is undeniable. Still, another facet of the fundamental ideology of compensatory education has been as persistent as philanthropic intentions: the tendency to define the nature of educational compensation and identify those to be compensated according to the needs of society and to the preconceptions of those devising educational programs, not on the basis of the needs of potential recipients. The same statutes that mandated schooling for servant children in colonial Massachusetts, for example, also defined its purpose: the need for all to "understand the principles of religion and the capital lawes [*sic*] of this country." Colonial Virginians likewise identified the aims of education in terms of their social conceptions and explicitly required that schools train "gentlemen." Even the colonies' *philosophe,* Benjamin Franklin, despite his clear distinction between learning and mere schooling, illustrated the tendency to define education in terms of society's needs when he proposed for colonial Pennsylvania a school system which would "obtain the Advantages arising from an increase of Knowledge, and prevent as much as may be the mischievous Consequences that would attend a general ignorance among us." For Franklin, as well as for other colonial Americans, education implied social and ethical learning in addition to intellectual development, and protection against the unspecified evils of ignorance.

Independence added political dimensions to the concept; as Benjamin Rush observed, "The business of education has acquired a new complexion"—that of a responsibility for ensuring a politically trustworthy electorate. And national leaders like Rush, Noah Webster, and Thomas Jefferson agreed that education should disseminate and perpetuate the ideals and values of the Revolution and the new Republic, not just purvey literacy. Indeed, both Rush and Webster advocated expanding that role well beyond the common school by creating a national university which would insulate potential leaders from pernicious European influences, and Rush recommended that a degree from such an institution be made a requisite for holding federal office. Thus, the compensatory function of public education, even at the university level, rapidly came to include forming a nation of politically homogeneous citizens, developing a national character premised upon the ideals of a political elite, and even striving to "convert men into republican machines." [2]

As the nation matured and expanded, so did awareness of the necessity for an educated citizenry and of the consequent political responsibilities of public schools, a concept Horace Mann himself expressed quite succinctly: "With thousands of voters, every year crossing the line of manhood to decree the destiny of the nation, without additional knowledge and morality, things must accelerate from worse to worse." Universal manhood suffrage obviously increased demands upon the school, particularly for those deficient in knowledge and morality. Simultaneously, New England and Pennsylvania workingmen's associations rallied to the support of universal public education and added an element that reflected new economic realities. To be sure, they articulated endorsement of Mann's ethical and political objectives and recognized the need for basic education in an expansive society. And they condemned the employment of children on moral grounds. But they also understood that the child in the classroom could not fill a position sought by an adult or depress an adult worker's wages. However, neither Mann nor Jacksonian workingmen but a young Whig, Abraham Lincoln, best summarized and integrated educational expectations of the era when he wrote in 1832:

I view education as the most important subject which we as a people can be engaged in. . . . I desire to see the time when education, and by its means, morality, sobriety, enterprise, and industry shall become much more general than at present.[3]

Like earlier Americans, Jacksonians revered and supported education, anticipating that it would benefit society as well as individuals and understanding that it had a special function for the less moral, sober, enterprising, or industrious among them. Moreover, like their predecessors, they willingly defined not only the needs society might reasonably expect general and compensatory education to fill but also the nature of education itself in terms of their own experiences.

Similar pragmatic attitudes and understandings remained operative after the Civil War. Educational activities of the Freedmen's Bureau and the philanthropic Slater and Peabody Funds on behalf of free blacks in the South—and of organizations like the American Missionary Society and the Freedmen's Aid Society before and during the conflict—are sufficiently familiar to require little elaboration. However, it is pertinent to observe that even in such benevolent efforts, utilitarian political, social, and economic understandings frequently motivated desires to compensate a deprived group through education. Indeed, the character of the education offered former slaves suggests a tendency to make learning a tool of necessity as defined by dominant elements in the society. To be sure, New England schoolmarms' futile efforts to instruct previously illiterate blacks in the niceties of the classics may have amused white southerners. But neither as naïve nor as entertaining were attempts to convince ex-slaves of their equality with whites, that former masters had achieved status only on the basis of stolen labor, or that the Republican party constituted the black man's sole political ally.[4] Their objectives were all too obvious.

Even after the demise of Radical Reconstruction and the apparent rejection of its policies, faith in the efficacy of compensatory education remained. For not a few Americans believed sincerely that the Civil War had resulted partly from defective southern educational systems and that failure to alter conditions invited recurrence of the conflict. To counter the possibility, Senator Henry Blair of New Hampshire offered a bill (which passed the U.S. Senate in 1884, 1886, and 1888) to provide federal aid to education on the basis of local illiteracy rates: where rates were high, funds would increase proportionately. Had effective educational institutions prevailed in the South, Blair argued, fanatics would have been unable to lead southern whites into war. Moreover, the senator insisted, new circumstances, particularly in northern cities, precipitated conditions there analogous to those in the antebellum South and provided opportunities for demagogues to exploit illiterate and politically ignorant voters. Clearly, Blair's bill embodied the principles of compensatory education, and just as clearly, educators echoed Blair in arguments supporting his bill: Universal suffrage and intelligent citizenship demanded universal education, economic and social progress depended upon an educated populace, and only an enlightened electorate could foil unscrupulous politicians permanently either in northern cities or the southern countryside. Even the usually staunch states' rights advocate, Jabez L. M. Curry, Confederate veteran and executor of both Slater and Peabody funds, supported the Blair Bill on precisely those grounds,[5] and municipal reformers employed a virtually identical rationale in their advocacy of altered political and educational structures.

It seems clear, then, even on the basis of a brief and selective synopsis, that the principle of compensation for deprived citizens who somehow deviated from norms of social or political expectations has been persistent in American educational thought. Moreover, it has been motivated by two major but often incompatible impulses: genuine idealism or philanthropy, on the one hand, and the desire to control and increase conformity to prescribed values, on the other. Thus, society rather than the individual has generally been the recipient of compensation. Indeed, tendencies to define and control compensatory education from above and to apply its principles on the basis of social and political utility have been among the most enduring threads in the historical fabric of public education.

Perhaps in preurban America the approach was beneficial and had a certain validity. For in 1782, when Crèvecoeur inquired into the nature of the new man—the American—a definitive answer based upon the existence of a relatively homogeneous population seemed at least possible. Despite already apparent diversity, the nation remained essentially rural-agrarian, and its citizens shared numerous common political, social, and economic assumptions, religious attitudes, and ethnic characteristics. A century later, however, that consensus no longer pertained. Urbanization, industrialization, and accelerated immigration had combined to increase diversity and specialization, to decrease ethnic and cultural homogeneity, and to erode the validity of rural-agrarian conceptions of American society. By 1880 bureaucratization had already expanded the gulf between government and the governed, particularly in cities, and only with increasing difficulty could leadership ascertain and evaluate educational and other needs of the masses of citizens. Accentuated by traditionalist, agrarianist, evolutionist, and elitist habits of thought, the separation simultaneously made bureaucratic control of education seem the most expedient means of reform and rendered it a singularly inappropriate approach in the increasingly pluralistic urban society of the Gilded Age.

Yet assumptions that provided the foundations for urban educational reform had changed less than actual conditions, and educators continued to act in conformity with the ideologies and practices of the past, identifying the social, moral, political, and intellectual deficiencies of city dwellers in terms of their own traditional, often rural-agrarian backgrounds and devising educational programs premised upon limited conceptions of urban society. To compensate for defective political understandings, educators sought not only to circumscribe the influence of the urban citizenry in school affairs but also to utilize the schools to inculcate the political morality educational leaders themselves defined. To remedy urban social and economic problems, educators proposed programs and institutions more relevant to the rural-agrarian experience than to the city, revealing their own antiurban biases. In more specifically compensatory educational efforts, similar impulses persisted. Attempts to alleviate economic dislocations through manual training more often reflected the values, priorities, and conceptions of those who developed policies than the realities of urban life. Similarly, specialized schemes intended to integrate immigrant children into the mainstream of American society were formulated with reference to the social, ethical, and ethnic assumptions of educators and virtually ignored positive elements of immigrant cultural life. Indeed, even the movement to graft the kindergarten onto the urban public school system, among the most benevolent and idealistic on nineteenth-century educational reforms, reflected tendencies to identify those to be compensated and to define the nature and purpose of compensation in reformers' rather than recipients' terms.[6]

Like their predecessors, Gilded Age urban educators included in their definition of education the compensatory principle dogmatically applied to segments of the urban population and aspects of urban life deemed morally, socially, politically, or economically defective. In fact, many educators considered the entire urban milieu in dire need of compensatory schooling. Despite obvious willingness—even eagerness —to provide it, however, the conditions under which educators operated hampered their ability to understand the city and the problems of its residents and predetermined the nature of educational responses to urban society. Never before had there been so many cities of such magnitude. Nor had there been such enormous, diverse, and concentrated school populations to educate. Dedicated to the tenets of the American faith in education and conditioned by their own ideologies, urban educators sought with severely limited resources, to compensate city children for losses presumably resulting from urbanization.

Not only the task's enormity and limitations imposed by inexperience and preconceptions impeded reform; the very nature of the bureaucratic structures created undermined effectiveness. Hierarchical systems of organization, despite apparent efficiency, accentuated the socioeconomic gap already existing between educational policy makers and their constituencies, established physical and psychological barriers to communication, impeded understanding, and therefore virtually precluded effective compensatory educational programs. Thus, the major results of urban educational reform in the Gilded Age are contradictory. The expediency and utility of impersonal educational bureaucracies can hardly be denied, at least from the organizational perspective. However, the resultant separation of schools from communities they supposedly served is equally apparent. Consequently, reform remained more superficial and mechanical than educational or, to paraphrase Michael B. Katz, only an illusion of reform.[7] Yet, it must be observed, in their willingness to prescribe compensatory programs while defining their content, nature, and recipients according to their own values and understandings, urban educators of the late 1800s departed little from previous American educational traditions.

However, there were laymen and professionals, whose vision of reform involved broader understandings than social control, traditional objectives, or rigidly bureaucratic school systems and whose efforts revealed a fuller conception of the purposes of education. Municipal reformers, including ladies of the New York City Public Education Association (PEA), made timid excursions toward realistic educational understanding by visiting working-class neighborhoods and schools in order to identify the specific needs of slum residents. Typically, however, such efforts lacked persistence; like many of the PEA ladies, reformers either found what they learned too repugnant, assessed their findings only with reference to their own systems of moral values, or simply deserted educational reform once the primary goal of political reorganization had been achieved.[8]

More significant than such capricious forays by municipal reformers were indirect influences of settlement workers upon the theory and practice of public education. Although conditions discovered in tenement districts also repelled settlers and middle-class backgrounds colored their interpretations as well, settlement workers most frequently remained in contact with ghetto dwellers long enough to comprehend the realities of slum life and accept, at least tentatively, values inherent in immigrant cultures. Indeed, settlers conscientiously studied tenement residents' lives, their social, economic, and cultural difficulties, and the impediments preventing successful integration into American society. Crime, thriftlessness, and alcoholism, they observed, less often resulted from dubious morality than from necessity, environment, or sheer desperation. Similarly, squalor and disease were products not only of the apathy of slum dwellers but also of the absence of even rudimentary sanitary facilities in the buildings they occupied but did not control. To be sure, corruption and vice abounded; yet among religious, social, and even political leaders in lower-class neighborhoods were to be found men of high integrity and ideals. If these and their followers could be attracted to community centers offering programs ranging from elementary economics and home management to social and cultural activities, settlement workers reasoned, the urban poor—native and immigrant alike—could learn to cope more effectively with their environment and even escape it. Moreover, despite sharp differences between their views of urban society and those of educators, many settlers defined their roles and the functions of the institutions they established as essentially educational and directly related to the work of the public school. Nor did they hesitate to preach the doctrine of the social function of the school to urban educators.[9]

Settlement workers' programs and philosophies and their insistence that many of the city's problems were indeed educational unquestionably influenced the attitudes of educational leaders. Pedagogical literature at the turn of the century reveals a growing concern for socioeconomic and

environmental conditions, frequent recommendations that
schools supplement efforts of the settlement, and even specific
suggestions such as installing shower facilities in schools to
combat hygienic problems in tenement districts.[10] If the settlement movement did not precipitate "revolution," it did substantially alter public education—through a specific program
of compensatory education, the kindergarten, not through
such subtle and indirect means as example, ideology, or
rhetoric.

Originally derived from the philosophical concepts of
Friedrich Froebel and initially adopted in the United States
in nursery schools for children of the well-to-do, the kindergarten rapidly evolved, in the hands of late nineteenth-century
settlement workers, into an institution directed toward the
social education of the urban poor and, through the settlers'
gospel of social education, into an important adjunct of the
public school. Even as principal speakers at NEA conventions,
settlers preached their homilies on the kindergarten and the
application of its principles at all school levels. The public
school could be made an effective instrument of compensatory
action for city children only by adopting new methods and
broadening conceptions of the social functions of education.
Education, regardless of the age or socioeconomic condition
of its recipients, could no longer be restricted to traditional
grammar, literature, mathematics, languages, and history.
Harris's "five windows of the soul" were by no means obsolete. But they were insufficient for the attainment of the true
goals of education: facilitating adaptation rather than conformity and thereby making "better scholars, better lives,
better homes, better citizens, and a better city."[11]

Furthermore, kindergarteners and settlers alike rejected
such traditional notions as belief in the chastening or character-
building qualities of poverty to which many educators adhered,
and argued that deprivation, particularly under urban-industrial
conditions, not only demoralized but also dehumanized. Nor
did they feel that the public school should focus solely upon
the child; as community-centered institutions, their objectives

should also include altering parental attitudes and specific socioeconomic conditions which resulted in working children, undernourishment, and absenteeism and perpetuated inherited ignorance. Socially conscious educators followed the lead of the kindergarteners and settlers in informing their colleagues of the implications of urban-industrial society—underscoring the relationship between poverty, ignorance, crime, and immorality and demanding that the public school diversify and expand to become a truly regenerative force in the urban community. To be sure, some kindergarteners and settlers regarded their programs as social panaceas, and elitist and paternalistic notions undeniably influenced them as well, but their impact upon urban education and its implications for future compensatory action through the schools were nevertheless significant.[12]

It would be naïve, of course, to assert that ideas emanating from the settlement and kindergarten movements precipitated radical revisions in educational thought in the Gilded Age. They did not; nor did anything else. Still, individual educational leaders did articulate and apply concepts closely allied to both movements. It is significant, however, that advocates of realistic revision in pedagogical ideologies and practices seldom emerged from urban school bureaucracies. Instead, they were individuals only tangentially connected with urban school systems or subordinate to them. The child psychologist President G. Stanley Hall of Clark University, for example, urged the application of sociological and psychological principles to education in order to augment the school's specific effectiveness as a social institution. Less theoretical than Hall, Principal Francis Wayland Parker of Cook County Normal School not only advocated and experimented with innovative teaching techniques but also called for a new definition of the social function of education. But neither Hall nor Parker (nor even Parker's disciple, John Dewey) concerned himself specifically with the problems of education in its urban setting.[13]

More explicitly urban-oriented responses to school problems emanated from sources not only external to the bureaucracy of the city system but also, on occasion, even from among nonprofessionals. Thomas Davidson, scholarly Scottish eccentric, erstwhile Fabian socialist, and supporter of Henry George (on the basis of his "sterling character," not the single-tax issue), in the New York City mayoral contest of 1886, provides one example. After delivering a single lecture to members of the Hebrew Educational Alliance on New York's Lower East Side, Davidson embarked upon a comprehensive educational campaign among the district's garment and sweatshop workers. A born dissenter and an incurable optimist, Davidson rejected any social theory that arbitrarily assigned inferior status to any man, and his educational activities reflected both his philosophy and his abiding respect for those he taught. Beginning in 1898 with an adult class in the humanities, he multiplied and expanded programs to include elementary and high school courses taught by adult students, neighborhood social centers, youth clubs, and the "Breadwinners' College," a series of cultural courses which evolved from his original lecture.[14]

Perhaps the best evidence of the appeal and effectiveness of Davidson's efforts is their survival. After the Scot's death in 1900, activities continued to expand under the direction of his former students and the auspices of the United Hebrew Charities.[15] However, no evidence indicates that his visionary experiment had any impact upon public educational thought or practice or even that professional educators recognized its existence. Nevertheless, programs such as Davidson's have a twofold significance. They provided models, though perhaps only by chance, for subsequent worker-oriented extension and continuation schools. But more important, they illustrated the potential of educational policies not premised upon traditional preconceptions or inhibited by the rigidity of the educational bureaucracy but sensitive to the needs and capacities of city residents themselves.

Similar sensitivity also motivated innovation among individuals in the lower echelons of urban school systems. Although cases are exceedingly difficult to document—the names, like those of plodding nonheroes in the ranks of a defeated army, defy detection—limited evidence does suggest that more effective reform in city schools might have resulted from the efforts of principals and teachers in individual schools rather than from policies devised and handed down from above. Life in close daily contact with city children and their parents, often under identical conditions, permitted a fuller understanding of the realities of urban society than that evolved by cloistered administrators whose limited contact with children and schools resulted in largely theoretical conceptions of education in the city.

Angelo Patri's career provides one example of the attempt to reform urban schools from within. An immigrant himself, Patri began to teach in the common schools of New York City in about 1895, attempting to support his family after an accident disabled his construction worker father. Very early in his career, he reacted against the traditionalism, sterility, rigidity, and general irrelevance of the city school and, influenced by Dewey's essay "Ethical Principles," determined to make at least his own classroom a place of social as well as academic learning. Despite difficulties, including the resistance of teachers, parents, and even students committed to educational traditionalism, Patri achieved a modicum of success. Later, as a principal, he converted his school into a community center concerned with matters ranging from student health to parent education and neighborhood beautification. Essentially because he shared their experience, Patri could comprehend the problems of immigrants, win the confidence essential to effective education, and devise programs which made the school an institution relevant to working-class life.[16]

Teachers, though restricted by subordinate status, also worked toward similar goals. As noted previously, many members of urban teaching staffs were less than sensitive to the needs of their charges. Yet others, like Patri, sought to understand city children and directed their teaching toward improving the lives and futures of their students. Even Joseph M. Rice tempered his critical assessment of urban schools with praise for the spirit of individual teachers who, hampered by minimal pedagogical training and impeded by rigid school systems, attempted to break the restraints of traditionalism in their classrooms. In numerous cities and schools, anonymous teachers labored to assist children in their adjustment to urban life, visited homes, shared problems, furnished guidance, and even purchased the clothing necessary to keep an impoverished child in school and out of the factory.[17] It is difficult to know or even to estimate the proportion of teachers willing to innovate in their classrooms, to give freely of their time, or to expend part of their meager salaries to furnish children with essentials. It can only be presumed that if a few cases have been recorded, many more existed. Yet even if such teachers were few, they remain significant. For their activities suggest that those who experienced the life of the community and the neighborhood, whether principals, teachers, or settlement workers, were by their very proximity more apt to identify accurately individuals and aspects of urban life in need of compensatory action. Moreover, their ability to establish the nature of compensation needed, clearly surpassed that of detached and often isolated bureaucrats and theoreticians.

It is equally apparent, however, that vital, appropriate, and broadly based reforms in urban education could not result from the activities of individual teachers or principals in isolated schools and classrooms. Nor could settlement workers, kindergartens, scholars, educational leaders, or concerned laymen precipitate permanent urban educational reform without massive institutional support. Although those closest to the city populace frequently identified deficiencies in traditional education and supplied appropriate but limited remedial responses, the avenues to organization and authority remained closed to them. And without institutions through which to channel their efforts or administrative authority to support them, compensatory educational programs initiated at lower levels seldom secured broad dissemination or wide acceptance. Local teacher organizations, which might otherwise have been effective instruments of reform, lacked the strength and cohesiveness for such an undertaking. Indeed, the only agencies that might have implemented meaningful change in city schools were those of educational bureaucrats: urban school systems locally and the NEA Department of Superintendence nationally. However, both of these institutions concentrated on structural rather than functional reform and, in the process, created organizational systems that effectively inhibited communication within the educational hierarchy and between educators and the urban community.

Furthermore, success in system building itself may have precluded effective innovation and reform. For not only did bureaucracies divorce administrators from the realities of urban life; they also effectively excluded many who understood the city dweller and his problems from influence in the schools. In the drive to recover control from ward politicians, educators eliminated an essential element of contact between city school systems and the community. Local school committeemen had been responsive to a constituency. But equally important, they frequently chose principals and teachers from among their constituents. The choice may have been improperly motivated, and those chosen ill-trained and less than competent. However, they had at least the virtues of familiarity with those they taught and understanding of their lives, qualities which no amount of normal school training could replace. As the ward boss often filled valid needs in the community, so, too, did local school committees and the local teachers they employed. Had urban educators diversified their efforts to include raising the professional standards and competence of such teachers, urban schools might have benefited.

Such was not the case, and the concentration of the educational bureaucrats upon structural reform resulted in dissipation of compensatory programs conceived and initiated at lower echelons. Conditioned by their own preconceptions of the city and urban society, committed to the organizational precepts of the bureaucracy, and divorced from the realities of urban life, educators could neither identify those in need of educational compensation nor implement appropriate compensatory policies. By isolating themselves within their own institutions, those who possessed the power and the authority to innovate effectively rendered themselves unable to form accurate assessments of urbanization and its impact. They therefore failed to create relevant urban educational institutions. Conversely, by being insulated from the sources of power and authority, those in the community who were most cognizant of urban life and its inherent problems and who could therefore respond effectively were unable to consolidate their efforts. As a consequence of both failures, urban educational institutions and practices dictated by the expedient of control from above persisted in city schools.

There can be little doubt that all of those who sought reform in urban education in the Gilded Age operated in the tradition of benevolent compensatory action. It is equally apparent, however, that only those in the upper ranks of the bureaucracy possessed sufficient prestige and authority to give permanence to their interpretation of the tradition. And the commitment of educators, not only to the concepts of centralization, efficiency, and control but also to the bureaucracy itself, institutionalized the less flexible and adaptive features of the compensatory tradition and in that rigid form bequeathed it to twentieth-century American education.

8

Urban Schools at the Close of the Century

> *As in the cities there is the greatest need for new ideals of social co-operation, so in the cities are to be found the best opportunities for realizing them.*
>
> —Charles DeGarmo

Like compensatory education, neither cities nor public schools were novel in the United States in the Gilded Age. Yet neither would be the same at the close of the nineteenth century as it had been 25 years earlier. For the city and the school had interacted with one another, with other institutions and ideas, and with physical changes in the American environment, and the interaction had wrought transformations in both. The change, however, particularly in the school, was more apparent than real. Cities had grown dramatically in the late 1800s and had thus imposed new and heavy demands upon urban schools. But in neither physical nor ideological development did education keep pace with urbanization. To be sure, new buildings rose, pedagogical principles and methods underwent rigorous scrutiny and reevaluation, and modern systems of school management emerged. Significant though such developments were, however, the function of the public school, particularly at the vital classroom level, differed little in 1900 from what it had been in 1875. What one author has called the "transformation of the school" might more accurately be termed the transformation of the *school system* as the phrase was applied to urban education in the Gilded Age.[1]

As has been seen, education's failure to adapt, except superficially, to urban needs cannot be ascribed to the ignorance of educators concerning changes occurring in the nation or to a paucity of interest. They knew and were concerned that American cities were growing rapidly, that the sources of growth involved migration from the countryside, immigration from abroad, and less tangible but already apparent factors such as declining infant mortality in cities. Moreover, educators recognized not only the shifting of the demographic balance toward urban dominance but also that the needs of urban education were growing even more rapidly than cities themselves. Indeed, as early as 1881, studies by the U.S. Bureau of Education gave statistical proof of that fact. In that year, 251 cities accounted for 17 percent of the nation's population and 26 percent of its average daily school attendance. Moreover, those same cities expended an aggregate of 33 percent of the nation's school money and controlled 49 percent of its school property.[2] With such precise analyses at their disposal, American educators can hardly be classed as uninformed. Nor does even the existence of such studies suggest disinterest. Yet twenty years later—indeed fifty years later—educators were struggling with the tangible problems the study illustrated. At the turn of the century, despite building programs and a spate of attendance and child labor laws, city school facilities remained woefully inadequate, and absenteeism and child labor, though diminished, remained major problems.

Nor were educators and educational reformers markedly more successful in adapting the ideological foundations of education to urban-industrial society or in creating a truly professional teaching force. Discussions and debates concerning pedagogical theories and methods abounded—frequently stimulated by concentrations of teachers in cities—but little indicates that such considerations had significant impact upon the classrooms of city schools. And if the evidence left by contemporary educators and critics is accepted, both content and methodology remained basically sterile at the end of the

century, changed only slightly with the passing of a generation. One must search diligently to discover records, aside
from the public-relations-oriented documents produced by
school system officials themselves, of any major progressive
trend in Gilded Age city schools. Despite expansions of common school curricula, including such appendages as manual
training and natural science, purposes and methods of urban
education remained for the most part bound by tradition.
Although the concept of individualism permeated educational
rhetoric, goals remained social harmony and control rather
than individual adaptation to a changing socioeconomic environment. Indeed, the rigidity and ossification inherent in
urban educational systems not only impeded implementation
of potentially beneficial programs aimed at the individual but
also limited innovation and creativity within the systems themselves. Only with the widespread acceptance—and frequent
misinterpretation—of John Dewey's principles in the twentieth century, did education begin to recognize and accept its
social role in the city.

Much of what has been said of curricula and of educational principles may be applied with justice to the teaching
profession as well. Despite the undeniable contributions of
individual teachers to the education of city children, the
pedagogical skills of most were archaic at best and methods
consisted of rote memorization of isolated facts and, above all,
rigid discipline. It is not surprising, however, that proficiency
in either pedagogical skill or academic mastery should be
rare. Unprecedented urban growth had made equally unprecedented demands upon city schools and consequently upon the
numbers of teachers required to staff them. As a result of
those demands, as well as of political manipulation, untrained
and even semischooled teachers filled the gaps, and at least
partially relieved pressures upon urban schools. Although un-
documentable, it is likely also that many thus pressed into
service became effective teachers whose sympathy and understanding overcame deficiencies in formal training. It is equally
likely that among the unforeseen results of the drive to

centralize school systems and strip them of political influence was the exclusion of such individuals from the teaching service and the consequent expansion of the gap between the public school and the urban community.

Originally intended as a means to improve standards and insure competence, the circumscription of members of the working classes from teaching also initiated problems with which urban educators continue to struggle. Teacher-training institutions and their faculties have, since the Gilded Age, become increasingly oriented toward the values and concepts of the so-called middling elements of American society. Thus, fewer and fewer teachers reflect anything resembling the cultural understandings of the urban working classes. Morover, suburbanization has further reduced contacts between social classes, and teachers drawn extensively from the suburban middle classes have little understanding of the needs of urban communities and even less desire to teach in them. When they do accept positions in urban schools, they depart as soon as possible, impelled by training or biases toward suburban schools. The inevitable consequence is that urban schools, already less well equipped than those in the suburbs, also become less well staffed. So pressing has the need become for teachers specifically trained to serve in urban schools that Dean Harry N. Rivlin of the School of Education at Fordham University has identified it as the primary problem to be solved if there is to be "a new era in urban education, rather than a new error."[3]

Not all urban-related changes in the teaching profession warrant negative assessment, however. Indeed, the very conditions that forced untrained men and women into city classrooms and fragmented relationships between school and community also drew attention to the demand for massive teacher preparation and allowed the creation of institutions for that purpose. Although neither normal schools nor in-service institutes originated in urban centers, concentrations of teachers and more adequate transportation in cities increased their effectiveness and expanded their scope. Minimal though the impact of initial efforts proved to be, both the identification of the need for increasing numbers of trained teachers and the conditions for the fulfillment of it are positive contributions upon which professionalism would be built in the twentieth century. Nevertheless, despite those contributions, nothing resembling a true teaching profession emerged in the Gilded Age in terms of either training and performance, monetary rewards, or status and privilege. To this generalization, the city administrator provides the sole visible exception.

The exception, however, is singularly important. For it integrates with the most permanent and significant change wrought in American schools by urban reform efforts of the late nineteenth century: the centralized, bureaucratically organized city school system. Whether the professional administrator caused or resulted from the change is a fruitless topic for debate. In fact, both are true. Reacting to inefficient and partisanly political urban school operation, dynamic educators exerted themselves to create efficient city school systems managed by experts. In the process, they outlined, constructed, and established permanent organizational patterns which—along with their defects—would become models for nearly every school district in the nation, urban and rural alike. The modern educational system resulted from the concerted effort of determined educators, dominating the NEA and cooperating through its Department of Superintendence. But despite its obvious unity of purpose, the campaign cannot be considered an intrigue or cabal. Initially neither well defined nor carefully organized, educational administrative reform paralleled municipal reform in numerous ways, frequently included municipal reformers themselves, and thus reflected the *Zeitgeist* of the era rather than a conspiracy to subvert control of the schools. Both movements derived motivation from the urban milieu itself, both responded to inefficiency, corruption, and the absence of expertise in the conduct of city affairs, and both predicated reform upon principles of organization, centralization, and control in the hands of competent administrators. As municipal reformers sought solutions to urban problems through reorganizing municipal governments, educators hoped to achieve their ends by restructuring city school systems. Morover, both movements presumed that the ultimate goal, social reform, could best be attained by the oblique thrust of institutional change rather than a frontal assault. And both accepted the necessity of good men to administer the systems they created.

It is not entirely accurate, as frequently has been asserted, to say that late nineteenth-century reformers sought governments of laws, not men. In reality they wanted both: good laws *and* good men, sound institutions and individuals of high moral and professional caliber to administer them efficiently. And in definitions of the sort of men for that task, educational and municipal reformers revealed additional ideological similarities: adherence to strongly elitist or paternalist notions, conviction of the superior validity of their values and conceptions of society, and certainty of their right and duty to provide the leadership necessary for social progress. Methods reflected those convictions; none rejected democracy, but nearly all redefined its meaning and its implications. By substituting citywide elections for ward-level contests, by decreasing the number of elective offices in favor of appointive ones, and by imposing civil service systems oriented to their own values and conceptions, municipal and educational reformers expected to secure better government, better officials, better schools, and thereby a better urban society. In the process, however, both frequently contracted the parameters of democracy in the city.

Urban educators made their answer to the question "Who shall rule at home?" eminently clear. Whether stimulated by a sense of duty, a conviction of superiority, or simple affinity for efficiency, reformers understood that authority ought to reside with men of obvious moral and intellectual fitness not unlike themselves. And in establishing criteria for fitness, Gilded Age educators learned from their own era: from science and technology, from predominant philosophies and the ideology of Progress, and especially from the apparent success of business and industry. However, business principles had greater utility for urban educators than simply identifying fit and able men; the tenets of efficiency, authority, and rationalization provided the rationale to which educators committed themselves. Once defined, the commitment became permanent and central in twentieth-century educational administrative doctrine, as Ellwood P. Cubberly's advice in 1916 attests:

The principles of good corporation organization need to be applied to educational affairs and boards of school directors need to assume more the position of a board of directors of a large corporation, giving to their executive officers the authority which corporation directors give to their presidents and superintendents.[4]

The principles Cubberly outlined have provided the foundation for urban school systems throughout the nation, and the bureaucracy they imply has become a major source of current school problems, an unfortunate legacy of educational developments in the Gilded Age.

If current educational literature is a criterion, among the most pressing needs in twentieth-century urban education is "a reform of a reform," one directed toward dismantling the bureaucracies erected in the late 1800s. Although holding educators of that era culpable for present problems would be an injustice, it is undeniable that circumstances resulting from their policies underlie numerous current difficulties. By limiting participation in school affairs, they unwittingly furthered the divorce of the school from the community, and ensuing generations have failed to heal the breach. Recent scholars find that lack of communication between school administrators and boards of education, on the one hand, and inner city schools and the populations they serve, on the other, remains prevalent, and that concern for the education of the middle-class student, the suburban child, typically permeates higher echelons of the educational structure. In fact, it has been argued that although local control of education has long been an American tradition, "The tragedy is that a large segment of our population has never enjoyed the privilege," and that solutions to city school problems demand a return to systems based upon representative bodies not unlike ward school boards eliminated in the Gilded Age.[5] That innovation, if innovation is the appropriate word, might indeed not only preserve links to the community but also capitalize upon positive features of the centralized system.

Barriers between school and community recently have begun to fall, principally as a consequence of the civil rights revolution and community action programs, but many educators continue to believe that accelerated decentralization constitutes the essential first step toward effective—rather than simply efficient—urban schools. Indeed, even the NEA, supported by the American Federation of Teachers (AFT) and local teachers' associations, has become an important advocate of decentralization as a means toward restoring interchange between cities and their schools, and many cities have begun to move in that direction. Although some support decentralization only tentatively and find it too simplistic a solution, particularly where suburbanization has shifted economic strength from the center city, most agree that some modification of the bureaucratic urban educational structure is essential.[6]

It is increasingly apparent that as twentieth-century educators attempt to cope with city school problems, they are forced to concern themselves with the historical perspective, the bureaucracies and ideologies of the Gilded Age, as one recent comment indicates:

The prevailing pattern of public school organization in most cities has its roots in nineteenth-century assumptions that the school must be independent of surrounding institutions, that suitable education will take place when students are divided equally among available teachers, and that a lay board can direct operations in accord with the public will.

Such assumptions not only have become the dominant bases for city school administration but also have rendered schools increasingly rigid, making innovation difficult at best and frequently discouraging it entirely.[7]

Because bureaucracies have grown in size and complexity,

because the bureaucratic concept has been generally accepted as the epitome of urban school efficiency, and because the system has frequently become top-heavy with its own vested interests, change is inhibited. Indeed, even arguments of those who assert that flexibility does exist, if only at the classroom level, tend to support the conclusion that room for creative maneuver within existing systems is minimal. As a result of the perpetuation and extension of reforms instituted in the Gilded Age, urban schools continue to operate, "administratively and pedagogically, as if [they] were somewhere in the middle of Siberia, or in a rural hamlet of self-sufficient farmers." Those who control schools continue to discuss teaching children to live in the world but have minimal knowledge of the real world in which urban children live.[8] Although the tone of such general indictments is perhaps too severe, the frequency with which they occur leaves little doubt concerning their essential validity.

Yet another process with roots in the Gilded Age, suburbanization, has further aggravated and complicated the problem. The population shift from center cities has not been an explicitly educational phenomenon. Nevertheless, it has seriously affected urban schools. The process of urban fragmentation begun with innovations in transportation technology in the late 1800s has all but invalidated Francis Wayland Parker's definition of the common school as the meeting ground for all classes of Americans. For all no longer share schools equally, even when de jure racial segregation is not a factor. The continuing flight of the upper and middle classes to the suburbs and to residential rings surrounding cities also has had a direct economic impact upon inner city schools. More than this, it has altered the basic economic and racial character of inner city school populations, further widened the gulf between those who control schools and those who attend them, and shaped the attitudes of all classes toward public education. The wealthy who have greatest access to authority over urban schools send their own children to suburban or private institutions and therefore have little immediate or personal interest in those of the inner city. The suburban middle classes whose needs and values are already reflected in public schools wish to preserve them as they are and resent the use of their tax money for educational facilities in the center city. The increasingly nonwhite lower classes who populate inner cities and who have the greatest need for effective public education sense the irrelevance of the system to their lives and therefore resent it. Simultaneously, those who most need the school are also frequently the least potent politically and the least well equipped to evaluate the quality of the education their children receive. Consequently, antagonisms and even violence have plagued attempts to solve city school problems.[9]

Although the assessment thus far made of Gilded Age urban school reform and its implications is essentially negative, it should be construed neither as an impeachment of reformers nor as a denunciation of their basic motives. Urban educators in the nineteenth century cannot be held entirely accountable for conditions in urban society in the twentieth. Nor can it be denied that their principles were essentially valid and their goals mainly benevolent. The major criticism involves the shortsighted *means* by which reformers sought to change the schools and their failure to commit themselves to the city or understand the broad implications of urbanization, a fault that weakened potentially significant steps toward adapting American education to urban-industrial society. As a consequence of that failure, the reformers' record is a mixed one.

To be sure, organizational reform did bring a semblance of order to a previously chaotic situation, and the creation of centralized, bureaucratic urban school systems did facilitate the rise of talented and dynamic educational leaders to positions of influence. Yet the cost was considerable. Highly centralized school systems contracted democracy in urban education, circumscribed those most familiar with the city, and thereby impaired realistic reform. Although the systems expanded opportunity for some, they contracted it for others. Centralization necessarily implied control from above, and eliminating ward representation effectively excluded members of the working classes from participation in school affairs and also closed one avenue of social, occupational, and political mobility to them. Furthermore, bureaucracies became progressively more rigid and those who managed them more inclined to equate efficiency with effectiveness and change with disorder. Despite these costs, however, school centralization failed to eliminate political influences from education; it only changed their nature.

The record of reformers' efforts to capitalize upon the educational potential of the city is similarly mixed. Urban concentrations gathered unprecedented numbers of teachers in close proximity and frequent contact and thus facilitated the beginnings—but only the beginnings—of an embryonic profession. The opportunity remained unexploited until the twentieth century, but it is significant that the foundations were laid in the cities of the nineteenth. Similarly, concentration focused attention on numerous other problems extending well beyond city boundaries to affect village and rural schools as well. For the first time, the transportation of pupils, the provision of free textbooks and supplies, and the inclusion of vaccination and other hygienic services in the schools emerged in pedagogical and legislative discussions with significant regularity, and cities most frequently provided the forums for their debate. Although the debates frequently terminated far short of broad practical implementation, it is well to remember that the innovations that did occur in American education were essentially urban products and that cities set precedents for school systems modern in more than bureaucratic structure.

Further nineteenth-century urban precedents have had similar long-range—and similarly mixed—implications for education and merit at least passing attention. Massive educational expenditures, for example, on both per-pupil and overall bases, have distinct origins in Gilded Age cities. Resistance persists, but school expenses have soared, without commensurate tangible results. Indeed, growing bureaucracies themselves consume inordinate proportions of expanding revenues for administrative staffs, facilities to accommodate them, and programs that, like manual training, prove costly but less than effective. Moreover, funds frequently have been funneled into administrator's pet projects—experimental programs, demonstration schools, and the like—which produce few tangible benefits because they can be applied neither on a massive scale nor within existing institutional frameworks. Thus, the urban school bureaucracy, as a consequence of its detachment from the realities of city school problems and its growing inbred rigidity, has ultimately contributed to the inefficiency it was intended to eliminate. The complaint remains, as it was in the Gilded Age, lack of "clearly discernible results," despite constantly increasing expenditures.[10]

And the continuing influence of suburbanization aggravates fiscal problems. The middle-class exodus which began in the late 1800s has left inner city schools economically and politically impoverished. Seriously reduced tax bases coupled with the disinterest of the wealthy and the resentment of the middle classes, who together control both fiscal power and educational policy, has left the urban school in desperate straits. The bulk of educational capital flows not to destitute inner city schools still using half-century-old buildings but rather to the equally needy suburban schools where new structures already are inadequate for expanding populations.[11] Yet the principle of massive spending remains—along with its flaws, failures, and inconsistencies, for current educators to contend with.

As urbanization influenced and modified the principle of public spending for general education, it also affected the concept of expenditure for specifically compensatory education, and with equally inconsistent results. Such publicly financed programs as manual training, kindergartens, business education, Americanization, and the schooling of mental and physical defectives all have important origins in late nineteenth-century cities. However, insufficient understanding, inappropriate motivations, and bureaucratic control frequently debilitated potentially significant adaptive educational programs.[12] The lack of insight, for example, which resulted in imposing the craftsmanship ethic on manual training and rejecting immigrant cultures in Americanization seriously impaired the effectiveness of numerous other programs.

Moreover, deficient understanding—comprehensible under conditions in the Gilded Age—has become institutionalized in educational bureaucracies and thus produces results contravening the increased mobility compensatory policies originally intended. Candidates for compensation continue to be identified less on the basis of real need and actual potential than in terms of educators' stereotyped assumptions concerning family, socioeconomic, or racial backgrounds. Consequently, compensatory education often has become the hallmark of the terminal student, the real or potential drop-out, or the simply "dumb," and the result more often has been increased social rigidity rather than mobility. Indeed, it may be argued with some justice that those most frequently compensated under present conditions are those least in need. For textbooks, teachers, and curricula—even in inner city schools—remain oriented toward the needs and assumptions of the suburban, middle-class, academically motivated sector of American society.[13] Such failures notwithstanding, however, it is well to remember that cities not only demonstrated needs for compensatory educational action and set precedents for its inclusion in public school curricula but also continue to provide conditions and resources—frequently overlooked—for its successful implementation.

Despite the educational possibilities present in cities and their occasional recognition by nineteenth-century educators, including Charles DeGarmo who found there "the greatest need for . . . new ideals of social co-operation . . . [and] . . . the best opportunities for realizing them,"[14] the potential, for the most part, remained unfulfilled. As a consequence of failure to recognize their opportunities, lack of understanding of the nature of urbanization, and frequent antipathy toward urban life, most educators concentrated upon structural rather than functional reforms. They expended their energies upon the physical, overt manifestations of urbanization rather than the real source of city problems, the basic inherent differences between urban and rural life. Thus, many urban educational difficulties of the nineteenth century were perpetuated in the twentieth. Moreover, their detachment from the urban community permitted educators to operate on the virtually unchallenged assumption that their own standards and values were not only the best but also universal, making meaningful change in the schools difficult.

Although there were positive results of educational reform in the Gilded Age, on balance, as a consequence of conditions in the cities and educators' attitudes toward them, both immediate and long-range consequences were essentially negative. The problems with which those educators struggled continue to confront the current generation. Indeed, a question raised at the close of the period has a decidedly modern ring:

Can we reduce the amount of money invested in drugs, prisons, and battleships, and [by turning it toward education and schools,] make a condition of civilization in which these things will not use so great a part of the energy and creative force of life?[15]

The same question might well be asked in the late twentieth century, principally as a consequence of earlier educators' inability to comprehend and grapple with more than the superficial manifestations of urbanization.

Paradoxically, nineteenth-century educators' failures emanate from two patterns of thought, apparently opposed but frequently present in the same individuals. For schoolmen of the Gilded Age were at once intellectual traditionalists and modernists. Traditionalism resulted in fruitless efforts to analyze, understand, and solve problems resulting from novel conditions in terms of obsolete standards and values. Traditional curricula, many educators believed, contained the moral and character-building elements necessary to bring order to an apparently disoriented society. Commitments to the rural-agrarian past revealed themselves in the educational mystique of nature and responses to socioeconomic dislocations with craftsmanship-oriented manual training programs.[16] Moreover, certainty of the moral superiority of the farm and rural life resulted in ambivalence or outright hostility toward cities and those who inhabited them. And traditional faith in education as a panacea permitted unwarranted complacency concerning the need for radical changes in the urban school.

Intellectual modernism supported this complacency. Tenets of evolutionist thought impelled educators toward faith in the abstract concept of Progress and the conviction that highly organized and sophisticated school systems guided by capable men would eliminate faults and insure improvement. Nor did the institutional or social facets of Spencerian doctrines cast doubt upon the soundness or general efficacy of their policies and programs. Commitment to Progress frequently blinded educators to the realities of urban life and obscured the necessity for schools to become instruments of change. Indeed, their modernism was a conservative rather than a dynamic creed, one that found assurance of social regeneration in the scientific and technological advances of their age.

These two patterns of thought merged with the growing rigidity of the bureaucracies educators had created and with centripetal tendencies in society to separate educators from the schools and from urban populations and to hamper judgments concerning the process of urbanization itself. Moreover, conditions did little to challenge the assumption that all was well as long as the machine functioned smoothly or to call into question the bureaucracy's legitimacy. Consequently, reforms instituted by Gilded Age urban educators altered city schools only superficially and assured perpetuation of apparently efficient organizational structures, along with their weaknesses and the numerous problems they could not solve. To be sure, remedies the educators implemented did possess a certain validity. Chaotic school systems could profit from more efficient management. Parks, contact with nature, and provisions for recreation undoubtedly improved the esthetic quality of cities and enhanced the lives of those who lived and attended school in them. Economic conditions did demand compensatory educational programs such as manual training. The failure of reform involves the erroneous assumption that any of these programs—or even all of them together—could solve the problems of city schools. And that assumption emanated from the deficient understandings educators brought to their analysis of the process of urbanization.

Merle Curti has suggested that educators have always regarded the school as a social institution but have neglected to develop the school system "in reference to other institutions, or on the basis of a realistic analysis of social actualities and social needs."[17] That assessment has particular validity for educators' responses to urbanization in the Gilded Age. Although it is apparent from what they said and wrote that educators were aware of urbanization, it is equally clear that they did not understand it as a social or economic process and responded principally to its external physical manifestations. Consequently, they reacted with piecemeal programs such as manual training or nature study rather than a vigorous reorientation of urban educational institutions. Only in their response to administrative and organizational problems did educators achieve significant success.

Ironically, that accomplishment ultimately impeded real progress. Educators failed not only to limit and define the objectives of public education in urban society appropriately but also to develop clear understandings of or commitments to urbanization and its educational potential. The failures may be mitigated, of course. In the Gilded Age, urbanization was a novel and astonishingly rapid process for which experience provided neither models nor precedents. Yet there were those in the late nineteenth century—including DeGarmo, Patri, Davidson, settlement workers and kindergarteners, and many individual teachers—who did articulate clear understandings of the implications of urbanization and who expressed their ideas lucidly and emphatically to their colleagues.[18] However, the responses of professional educators to the alternatives offered remained minimal and essentially peripheral. That failure to respond lies close to the heart of many of the crises that currently confront schools in the cities of the United States.

Notes

Abbreviations Used in Notes

AM	*Atlantic Monthly*
APNEA	*Journal of the Addresses and Proceedings of the National Education Association*
AQ	*American Quarterly*
CHQ	*California Historical Quarterly*
ER	*Educational Review*
GPO	Government Printing Office
HEQ	*History of Education Quarterly*
HER	*Harvard Education Review*
HM	*Harper's Monthly*
HW	*Harper's Weekly*
JAH	*Journal of American History*
JEH	*Journal of Economic History*
JNH	*Journal of Negro History*
JSH	*Journal of Southern History*
MM	*McClure's Magazine*
MVHR	*Mississippi Valley Historical Review*
NAR	*North American Review*
OM	*Overland Monthly*
PHR	*Pacific Historical Review*
PMHB	*Pennsylvania Magazine of History and Biography*

PNQ	*Pacific Northwest Quarterly*
PS	*Pedagogical Seminary*
PSQ	*Political Science Quarterly*
RMSSJ	*Rocky Mountain Social Science Journal*
SF	San Francisco (with newspapers)
SM	*Scribner's Magazine*
UE	*Urban Education*
USAR	*Annual Report of the United States Commissioner of Education*
WW	*World's Work*

Sources with single-word titles are not abbreviated.

INTRODUCTION

1. Charles J. P. Bourget, *Outre-Mer: Impressions of the Americans* (New York: Scribner's, 1895), 276.
2. Henry J. Perkinson, *The Imperfect Panacea: American Faith in Education, 1865–1965* (New York: Random House, 1968), chap. 1.
3. See, for example, Richard Hofstadter, *Anti-Intellectualism in American Life* (New York: Knopf, 1960), chap. 5, and John William Ward, *Andrew Jackson: Symbol for an Age* (New York: Oxford University Press, 1955).
4. Lawrence A. Cremin, *The Genius of American Education* (New York: Vintage, 1965), 4; Mann, *Twelfth Annual Report of the Board of Education* (Boston: n.p., 1849), 59.
5. Perkinson, *Imperfect Panacea.*
6. Bettie A. Dutton, "Discipline in the Elementary School," *APNEA* (1889), 487–488; italics in original.
7. Examples of the tendency to write educational history on the basis of the ideal rather than the real are numerous. See, for example, Lewis F. Anderson, *History of Manual and Industrial School Education* (New York: Appleton, 1926); Ernest E. Bayles and Bruce L. Hood, *Growth of American Educational Thought and Practice* (New York: Harper & Row, 1966); Ellwood P. Cubberly, *Public Education in the United States* (Boston: Houghton Mifflin, 1934); William E. Drake, *The American School in Transformation* (Englewood Cliffs, N.J.: Prentice-Hall, 1955).

   For more critical and balanced analyses, see Sol Cohen, *Progressives and Urban School Reform: The Public Education Association of New York City, 1895–1954* (New York: Columbia University Press, 1964); Lawrence A. Cremin, *The Transformation of the School: Progressivism in American Education, 1876–1957* (New York: Knopf, 1961); Michael B. Katz, *The Irony of Early School Reform: Innovation in Mid-Nineteenth Century Massachusetts* (Cambridge, Mass.: Harvard University Press, 1968); M. B. Katz, *Class, Bureaucracy, and the Schools: The Illusion of Educational Change in America* (New York: Praeger, 1971); David B. Tyack (ed.), *Turning Points in American Educational History* (Waltham, Mass.: Blaisdell, 1967); Robert H. Wiebe, "The Social Functions of Public Education," *AQ,* XXI (Summer 1969), 147–164; Rush Welter, *Popular Education and Democratic Thought in America* (New York: Columbia University Press, 1962); Stanley K. Schultz, *The Culture Factory: Boston Public Schools, 1789–1860* (New York: Oxford University Press, 1973), and Perkinson, *Imperfect Panacea.*

8. Duane Doty and William Torrey Harris, *A Statement of the Theory of Education in the United States of America as Approved by Many Leading Educators* (Washington, D.C.: GPO, 1874), 13.

9. Dewey, *The School and Society* (Chicago: University of Chicago Press, 1899), 18; Cubberly, *Changing Conceptions of Education* (Boston: Houghton Mifflin, 1909), 17.

10. The terms "educator" and "reformer" are used to designate specific groups. Educator applies not to teachers or pedagogical theoreticians but to those involved in the administrative reform of city schools. Reformer designates lay allies in that effort. For stylistic purposes, "educational reformers" is used to include both groups collectively.

11. *USAR* (1903/04), II, 1729.
   In 1890, only about 200,000 students enrolled in public high schools (6.7 percent of the 14-to-17-year-old population), and only 10 to 20 percent ever graduated. See Tyack, *Turning Points,* 355.

12. Francis Wayland Parker, "The School of the Future," *APNEA* (1891), 86–87.

13. Katz, *The Irony of Early School Reform,* 218.

14. See, for example, Sam Bass Warner, Jr., *Streetcar Suburbs: The Process of Growth in Boston, 1870–1900* (Cambridge, Mass.: Harvard University Press, 1962), Richard C. Wade, "Urbanization," in C. Vann Woodward (ed.), *The Comparative Approach to American History* (New York: Basic Books, 1968), 187–205, and Robert H. Wiebe, *The Search for Order, 1877–1920* (New York: Hill & Wang, 1967), chap. 5.

CHAPTER ONE

1. John D. Philbrick, *City School Systems of the United States* (Washington, D.C.: GPO, 1885), 10; *USAR* (1881/82), cix.
2. Donald J. Bogue, *The Population of the United States* (New York: Free Press, 1961), 30, 34, 69, 103, 307. For a convenient summary of urban growth during the period, see Blake McKelvey, *The Urbanization of America, 1860–1915* (New Brunswick, N.J.: Rutgers University Press, 1963), 20–30. Statistical volumes of *USAR* provide useful data on the growth of urban school populations. Between 1876 and 1905, for example, San Francisco's school-age population grew from 46,238 to 98,178; Chicago's from 110,184 to 489,197; New Orleans' from 69,093 to 96,543; Cleveland's from 43,342 to 114,393; and New York's from an estimated 375,000 to nearly one million. Other cities of over 50,000 reported similar trends.
3. Harris, "City School Systems," *USAR* (1894/95), I, 3; J. L. Pickard, "City Systems of Management of Public Schools," *APNEA* (1883), 69. See also Alexander Hogg, "The Problem of the Hour," *APNEA* (1889), 307–308; Henry Raab, "The Rural School Problem," *APNEA* (1892), 572, and N. Cropsey, "What Should the Public School Do for the Child?" *APNEA* (1896), 346.
4. *Statistical History of the United States from Colonial Times to the Present* (Stamford, Conn.: Fairfield, 1965), 213; F. W. Hewes, "The Public Schools of the United States," *HW*, XXXIX (November 23, 1895), 1113; William B. Shaw. "Compulsory Education in the United States, III," *ER*, IV (September 1892), 135–136; Moses Stambler, "The Effect of Compulsory Education and Child Labor Laws in New York City, 1897–1917," *HEQ*, VIII (Summer 1968), 203; Alzina P. Stevens, "Child Slavery in America," *Arena*, X (June 1894), 117–135; Philbrick, *City School Systems*, 186; Nicholas Murray Butler, editorial, *ER*, II (November 1891), 380.
5. *USAR* (1897/98), II, 1679; *USAR* (1891/92), II, 663; *USAR* (1885/86), 219; *USAR* (1899/1900), II, 2596–2597; Shaw, "Compulsory Education, III," 133, 140; Stevens "Child Slavery," 117.
6. Calvin M. Woodward, "At What Age Do Pupils Withdraw from the Public Schools?" *USAR* (1894/95), II, 1161–1170; Jacob Riis, "Children of the Poor," *SM*, XI (May 1892), 531–566; Dutton, "Discipline in Elementary Schools," 487.
7. W. C. Russell, "What Can Be Done to Secure a Larger Proportion of Educated Labor among Our Producing and Manufacturing Classes?" *APNEA* (1876), 262; *USAR* (1882/83), lxxvii.

8. James C. Boykin, "City School Systems," *USAR* (1891/92), II, 663; Lawton B. Evans, "The Factory Child," *APNEA* (1904), 245–246; *USAR* (1885/86), 219–220; Hogg, "The Problem of the Hour," 299–300; Nicholas Murray Butler, editorial, *ER*, II (November 1891), 380; Lucia Stickney, "The Homes of Our Downtown Children," *APNEA* (1899), 391; *USAR* (1883/84), lxxxv; Nicholas Murray Butler, editorial, *ER*, I (February 1891), 178.

9. Rice, "Our Public School Systems: Evils in Baltimore," *Forum*, XIV (October 1892), 147; Rice, "The Public Schools of St. Louis and Indianapolis," *Forum*, XIV (December 1892), 432–433; Rice, "The Public School System of New York City," *Forum*, XIV (January 1893), 617–618; Rice, "The Public Schools of Boston," *Forum*, XIV (February 1893), 754; J. H. Penniman, "Criminal Crowding of Public Schools, 7," *Forum*, XIX (May 1895), 292.

10. Helen M. Todd, "Why Children Work: The Children's Answer," *MM*, XL (April 1913), 69–70, 76–77; Jane Addams, "Foreign-Born Children in the Primary Grades," *APNEA* (1897), 108; Reuben Post Halleck, "Why Do So Many First-Year Pupils Leave High School?" *APNEA* (1905), 439.

11. *USAR* (1881/82), cx, cxiv; *USAR* (1901/02), II, 2347; *USAR* (1904/05), I, 185–186; Addams, "Child Labor," *APNEA* (1905), 260; *USAR* (1905/06), II, 1273; Stambler, "The Effect of Compulsory Education Laws," 205; Jacob Riis, *The Battle with the Slum* (New York: Macmillan, 1902), 231.

12. Riis, *How the Other Half Lives* (New York: Hill & Wang, 1957 [1890]), 135; *USAR* (1882/83), lxxiv; Philbrick, *City School Systems*, 155; J. H. Penniman, "Criminal Crowding of Public Schools, 2," *Forum*, XX (January 1896), 547.

13. *USAR* (1892/93), II, 1787; *USAR* (1898/99), II, 2497; *USAR* (1902/03), II, 1433; *USAR* (1877/78), lix-lxv; Philbrick, *City School Systems*, 156; *USAR* (1884/85), xlvii.

14. *USAR* (1882/83), xxx; *USAR* (1890/91), II, 1031–1079; *USAR* (1893/94), II, 1326–1349; *USAR* (1895/96), I, 1175–1198; E. H. Bradford and J. S. Stone, "School Seats," *USAR* (1898/99), I, 611–617; "Disease in Second Hand Books," *USAR* (1899/1900), II, 2548–2586; *USAR* (1904/05), I, 207; *USAR* (1891/92), II, 672; Rice, "Our Public School Systems: The Schools of Buffalo and Cincinnati," *Forum*, XIV (November 1892), 304; Rice, "The Public School System of New York City," 672; Penniman, "Criminal Crowding, 1," 289.

15. Riis, *The Battle with the Slum*, 346; Cohen, *Progressives and Urban School Reform*, chaps. 1 and 2; *USAR* (1891/92), II, 673.

16. Elizabeth M. Howe, "The Big Red Schoolhouse," *ER,* XX (October 1900), 260–267; S. A. Wetmore, "Boston School Administration," *ER,* XIV (September 1897), 116; Ellwood P. Cubberly, "The School Situation in San Francisco," *ER,* XIV (April 1901), 371.

17. Penniman, "Criminal Crowding, 1," 292–294; Howe, "The Big Red Schoolhouse," 260; Penniman, "Criminal Crowding, 2," 549.

18. Stewart, "Unsanitary Schools," 103; Rice, "The Public School System of New York City," 627.

19. Penniman, "Criminal Crowding, 1," 295; Stewart, "Unsanitary Schools," 110–112; *USAR* (1891/92), II, 671, 674; Penniman, "Criminal Crowding, 2," 549; Nicholas Murray Butler, editorial, *ER,* I (May 1891), 485–486; Aaron Gove, "Report of the Committee on City School Systems," *APNEA* (1896), 464; Marion F. Washburne, "The Educational Crisis in Chicago," *Arena,* XV (March 1896), 611–618. For an analysis of increasing educational expenditures, see Albert Fishlow, "Levels of Nineteenth Century Investment in Education," *JEH,* XXVI (December 1966), 418–432.

20. Howe, "Settlers in the City Wilderness," *AM,* LXXVII (January 1896), 118; Woods, *The City Wilderness: A Settlement Study* (Cambridge, Mass.: Riverside Press, 1898), 1–5, 7, 112–113. See also the provocative analysis in Sam Bass Warner, Jr., *The Urban Wilderness: A History of the American City* (New York: Harper & Row, 1973), chaps. 3, 4, 6, and 7; Henry S. Canby, *The Age of Confidence: Life in the Nineties* (New York: Farrar-Rinehart, 1934), 8–10; Robert M. Fogelson, *The Fragmented Metropolis: Los Angeles, 1850–1930* (Cambridge, Mass.: Harvard University Press, 1967), chap. 5; Bayrd Still, *Milwaukee: The History of a City* (Madison, Wisc.: State Historical Society of Wisconsin, 1948), 379; Blake McKelvey, *Rochester: The Quest for Quality, 1890–1920* (Cambridge, Mass.: Harvard University Press, 1956), chap. 2; Zane L. Miller, "Boss Cox's Cincinnati: A Study in Urbanization and Politics, 1880–1914," *JAH,* LIV (March 1968), 823–838; Humbert S. Nelli, *The Italians in Chicago, 1880–1930: A Study in Ethnic Mobility* (New York: Oxford University Press, 1970), chap. 2; Warner, *Streetcar Suburbs,* chap. 1 and *passim;* Wade, "Urbanization."

21. Philbrick, *City School Systems,* 5, 132; Evans, "The Factory Child," 245, 248–249.

CHAPTER TWO

1. Those employing over 1,000 were Philadelphia, Boston, and Brooklyn; those over 700 included St. Louis, Baltimore, and Chicago; over 500 were Cincinnati and San Francisco. Dozens of other cities employed over 100 teachers. See statistical volumes of *USAR*.

2. Tyack, *Turning Points*, 412; NEA Department of Classroom Teachers, *Local Organizations—A Manual for Leaders* (Washington, D.C.: NEA, 1937), 4.

3. Willard S. Ellsbree, *The American Teacher: Evolution of a Profession in a Democracy* (New York: American Book Co., 1939), 519–524, 526.

4. *Ibid.*, 458; N. S. Palmer, *Pension Systems for Public School Teachers* (Washington, D.C.: GPO, 1927), 4; Haley, "Why Teachers Should Organize," *APNEA* (1904), 147–149.

5. W. F. Phelps, "The Country School Problem," *APNEA* 1875), 13; Edward Olney, "The Country-School Problem," *APNEA* (1876), 38; Raab, "The Rural School Problem," 574–576; William H. Maxwell, "City School Systems," *APNEA* (1890), 447–469; G. Stanley Hall, "The Case of the Public Schools," *AM, LXXIV* (March 1896), 404–408; W. H. Maxwell, "Charter Provisions as Related to the Organization of School Systems," *APNEA* (1905), 219; "Confessions of Public School Teachers," *AM, LXXVIII* (July 1896), 97.

6. J. H. Smart, *Teachers' Institutes* (Washington, D.C.: GPO, 1885); Edgar B. Wesley, *NEA: The First Hundred Years* (New York: Harper, 1957), 87; *USAR* (1898/99), II, 1842; William C. Ruediger, *Agencies for the Improvement of Teachers in Service* (Washington, D.C.: GPO, 1911).

7. M. A. Newell, "Contributions to the History of Normal Schools in the United States," *USAR* (1898/99), II, 1740, 2263–2265; Ellsbree, *The American Teacher*, 153, 329; Wesley, *NEA* 16; J. W. Philbrick, "The Normal School Problem," *APNEA* (1871), 121; R. Edwards, "Normal Schools in the United States," *APNEA* (1876), 51; A. G. Boyden, "Distinctive Features of Normal School Work," *APNEA* (1886), 393.

8. Wesley, *NEA*, 49; *USAR* (1898/99), II, 1789; Tyack, *Turning Points*, 415; Ellsbree, *The American Teacher*, 314–315, 323; *APNEA* (1908), 735.

9. Newell, "Contributions," 2447–2464; Burke A. Hinsdale, "The Training of Teachers," in Nicholas Murray Butler (ed.), *Monographs in Education in the United States*, I (Albany:

J. B. Lyon, 1900), 368–379; Ellsbree, *The American Teacher,* 314.

10. *USAR* (1894/95), II, 1076; Tyack, *Turning Points,* 417; F. W. Atkinson, "The Teacher's Social and Intellectual Position," *AM,* LXXVII (April 1896), 537; Burke A. Hinsdale, "Pedagogical Chairs in Colleges and Universities," *APNEA* (1889), 560–563; Butler, editorial, *ER,* II (July 1891), 179–180.

11. *USAR* (1897/98), II, 1662–1691; *USAR* (1903/04), I, 463–519; F. W. Hewes, "The Public Schools of the United States," *HW,* XXXIX (November 9, 1895), 1068–1069; Hewes, "The Public Schools of the United States," *HW* (November 30, 1895), 1141; Ellsbree, *The American Teacher,* 433; Theodore R. Sizer, *Secondary Schools at the Turn of the Century* (New Haven, Conn.: Yale University Press, 1964), 42.

12. Sizer, *Secondary Schools,* 46; Rice, "Schools of Buffalo and Cincinnati," 295–296; Draper, "Common Schools in the Larger Cities," *Forum,* XVII (June 1899), 390; Rice, "The Public Schools of New York City," 626; Eliot, "Undesirable and Desirable Uniformity in Schools," *APNEA* (1892), 86.

13. Rice, "Schools of Buffalo and Cincinnati," 301–302, 309; Rice, "The Public Schools of Boston," 146; Rice, "The Public School System of Philadelphia," *Forum,* XV (March 1893), 31–32; Rice, "The Public Schools of St. Louis and Indianapolis," 430–431; Cubberly, "The School Situation," 370–371; Adele M. Shaw, "The Public Schools of a Boss-Ridden City," *WW,* VII (February 1904), 4465; Adele M. Shaw, "How Successful Are the Public Schools?" *WW,* IX (November 1904), 5480–5485; NEA, *Report of the Committee of Fifteen on Elementary Education* (Boston: New England Publishing Co., 1895), 3–42; Maxwell, "The Grammar School Curriculum," *ER,* III (May 1892), 473, 479–481; Canby, *The Age of Confidence,* 109–110; "Course of Study in Public Elementary Schools in Cities," *USAR* (1888/89), I, 373–387; *USAR* (1897/98), I, 869–871; Emerson E. White, "Isolation and Unification as Bases of Courses of Study," *USAR* (1895/96), I, 929–934; F. R. Morrison, "The Dark Side of the Picture," *ER,* XIV (November 1897), 383–387; Addams, "Foreign-Born Children," 112; J. L. Snyder, "Education for the Industrial Classes," *APNEA* (1898), 761–763; Dana F. White, "Education in the Turn-of-the-Century City: The Search for Control," *UE,* IV (July 1969), 178–180.

14. Hugo Münsterberg, *The Americans* (London: Doubleday, 1904), 379 and *American Traits* (Boston: Houghton Mifflin, 1901), chap. 2; "Confessions of Public School Teachers," 109–110; Rice, "The Public School System of New York City," 622.

15. Rice, "The Public School System of New York City," 619–620. A child's response, "A crooked line," rather than simply "A line," was unacceptable because it included the response the next child in line was expected to give.
Rice, "The Public Schools of Boston," 754; Rice, "The Public Schools of St. Louis and Indianapolis," 432–433; Rice, "Evils in Baltimore," 151–156; Rice, "The Public Schools of Buffalo and Cincinnati," 295–301, 306–308; Rice, "The Public School System of Philadelphia," 35; Rice, "The Public Schools of Chicago and St. Paul," *Forum*, XV (April 1893), 202–209.

16. Eliot, "Undesirable and Desirable Uniformity," 88; Dutton, "Discipline in Elementary Schools," 491; Adele M. Shaw, "The True Character of New York Public Schools," *WW*, VIII (December 1903), 4210–4215; Shaw, "How Successful Are the Public Schools?" 5480–5485.

17. Rice, "Why Teachers Have No Professional Standing—Some Suggestions to the National Education Association," *Forum*, XXVII (June 1899), 452–463; F. W. Atkinson, "The Teacher's Intellectual and Social Position," *AM* (April 1896), LXXVII, 536–537; Hall, "The Case of the Public Schools," 404; Ellsbree, *The American Teacher*, 551; Canby, *The Age of Confidence*, 114; Rice, "Evils in Baltimore," 148; Wesley, *NEA*, 397.

18. L. W. Chamberlain, *Women and Men in the Teaching Force* (Lexington, Kent.: University of Kentucky, 1937), 12. The figures for women in the interim decades are 57.2% in 1880, 65.5% in 1890, 70.1% in 1900, and 76% in 1905.
F. W. Hewes, "The Public Schools of the United States," *HW*, XXXIX (October 26, 1895), 1020; Solomon Schindler, "A Flaw in Our Public School System," *Arena*, VI (June 1892), 59–63.

19. Wesley, *NEA*, 286; Allen Johnson (ed.), *Dictionary of American Biography* (New York: Scribner's, 1928); *Who Was Who in America* (Chicago: A. N. Marquis, 1942); *The National Cyclopaedia of American Biography* (New York: James T. White, 1896–1906), and NEA, *Fiftieth Anniversary Volume* (Winona, Minn.: NEA, 1906) provide professional data for those who filled NEA offices.

20. Wesley, *NEA*, 48.

CHAPTER THREE

1. Pickard, "City Systems of Management," 69; Eaton, "Introduction," *USAR* (1876/77), lvi; Gove, "The Trail of the City Superintendent," *USAR* (1899/1900), I, 575.

2. Theodore L. Reller, *The Development of City Superintendency in the United States* (Philadelphia: the author, 1935), 34–35, 37.

3. *Ibid.*, 124–125, 196. Boston was an exception to the generalization; see Michael B. Katz, "The Emergence of Bureaucracy in Urban Education: The Boston Case, 1850–1884," *HEQ*, VIII (Summer 1968), 155–188, and (Fall 1968), 319–357.

4. *USAR* (1890/91), II, 982–998; *USAR* (1895/96), I, xx–xxi; Cubberly, *Public Education*, 309; Philbrick, *City School Systems*, 20–21; H. S. Jones, "Report of the Committee on City School Systems—Pupils: Classification, Examination, and Promotion," *APNEA* (1886), 276–282; Frank F. Bunker, *Reorganization of the Public School System* (Washington, D.C.: GPO, 1916), chap. 2.

5. Philbrick, *City School Systems*, 19; Cubberly, *Changing Conceptions*, 62–63. On Taylor, see Samuel Haber's perceptive *Efficiency and Uplift: Scientific Management in the Progressive Era, 1890–1920* (Chicago: University of Chicago Press, 1964), x–xii, 64–66, 72–74. See also Raymond E. Callahan, *Education and the Cult of Efficiency* (Chicago: University of Chicago Press, 1962).

6. Hinsdale, "City School Systems," *Dial*, XXV (October 16, 1898), 251. Hinsdale opposed rigid organization in 1877 and particularly graded schools; see Katz, "Emergence of Bureaucracy," 320–322.

7. Pickard, "City Systems of Management," 70; *USAR* (1881/82), lviii–lxii; Aaron Gove, "Duties of City Superintendents," *APNEA* (1884), 27; Henry P. Emerson, "Improvement of City School Systems," *APNEA* (1894), 121–128; Andrew S. Draper, "Organization of City School Systems," *Report of the Committee of Fifteen*, 75–94; A. S. Draper, "Plans of Organization for School Purposes in Larger Cities," *APNEA* (1894), 298–310. In *ER*, see the following: Aaron Gove, "City School Supervision—I," II (October 1891), 256–261; J. M. Greenwood, "City School Supervision—II," II (November 1891), 362–365; Thomas J. Baillett, "City School Supervision—III," II (December 1891), 482–486; Horace S. Tarbell, "City School Supervision—IV," III (January 1892), 65–69; W. T. Harris, "City School Supervision—V," III (February 1892), 167–172; A. S. Draper, "Plans of Organization for School Purposes in Larger Cities," VI (June 1893), 1–16; Albert P. Marble, "City School Administration," VIII (September 1894), 154–168; James C. Boykin, "Organization of City School Boards," XIII (March 1897), 232–249; Truman DeWeese, "Better City School Administration," XX (June 1900), 61–71. See also William H. Maxwell, "Charter Pro-

visions as Related to the Organization of School Systems,"
APNEA (1905), 214–223; Edward C. Eliot, "A Nonpartisan
School Law," *APNEA* (1905), 229; *Report of the Committee
of Fifteen,* 90; Philbrick, *City School Systems,* 18.

8. Gove, "Limitation of the Superintendent's Authority and of
the Teacher's Independence," *APNEA* (1904), 152–153, 155;
Maxwell, "Education for Efficiency," *APNEA* (1905), 59–67.
See also the NEA symposium titled "Means of Increasing the
Efficiency of Our Public School Work," *APNEA* (1905), 180–
194, and *USAR* (1905/06), II, 1286–1288. Philbrick, *City
School Systems,* 57; Pickard, "City Systems of Management,"
73; Wetmore, "Boston School Administration," 117; Gove,
"Trail of the City Superintendent," 572; Joseph M. Rice, "A
Plan to Free the Schools from Politics," *Forum,* XVI (De-
cember 1893), 500–507; "Powers of City School Boards with
Regard to School Sites and Buildings," *USAR* (1888/89), I,
579–587; Hinsdale, "City School Systems," 252.

9. The model synthesizes ideas contained in the following:
Charles W. Eliot, "A Good Urban School Organization,"
USAR (1902/03), II, 1356–1362; "Report of the Subcom-
mittee on the Organization of City School Systems," *USAR*
1893/94), I, 543–556; Gove, "Report of the Committee on
City School Systems," 464–470; Arthur H. Chamberlain,
"The Growth of Responsibility and Enlargement of Power of
the City School Superintendent," *University of California
Publications in Education,* III:4 (May 15, 1913), 362–395;
Ellwood P. Cubberly, *The Portland Survey: A Textbook on
City School Administration Based on a Concrete Study* (New
York: World Book, 1916); Cubberly, "The School Situation,"
364–381; Draper, "Common Schools in Larger Cities," 385–
397; Eliot, "A Nonpartisan School Law," 223–231; A. O.
Ernst, "The Movement for School Reform in Boston," *ER,*
XXXVIII (December 1904), 433–443; Elmer E. Brown and
others, *Report of the Commission to Study the System of
Education in the Public Schools of Baltimore* (Washington,
D.C.: GPO, 1911). Other sources cited herein have also con-
tributed to the model.

10. *USAR* (1895/96), 16–19; David C. Hammack, "The Cen-
tralization of New York's Public School System, 1896: A Social
Analysis of the Decision," (M.A. thesis, Columbia University,
1969), chap. 1 and *passim*; Katz, "The Emergence of Bureau-
cracy," 157–161, 328–338; Ernst, "The Movement for School
Reform in Boston," 435–438; Marvin Lazerson, *Origins of the
Urban School: Public Education in Massachusetts, 1870–1915*
(Cambridge, Mass.: Harvard University Press, 1971), 3–4.

11. Brown, *Report of the Commission,* 28–33; George D. Strayer,

"The Baltimore School Situation," *ER,* XLII (November 1911), 327-328; *Report of the Committee of Fifteen,* 90; Draper, "Plans of Organization," 305–306; L. H. Jones, "The Politicians and the Public School: Indianapolis and Cleveland," *AM,* LXVII (June 1896), 815–818, 820–822; Nicholas Murray Butler, editorial, *ER,* XIV (June 1897), 102–104; George S. Counts, *School and Society in Chicago* (New York: Harcourt, Brace, 1928), 36–38.

12. James M. Greenwood, "School Reminscences," *ER,* XXI (April 1901), 346–348; Eliot, "A Nonpartisan School Law," 224–226; Boykin, "Organization of City School Systems," 238–239; Cubberly, "The School Situation," 372–373; Lee S. Dolson, "The Administration of San Francisco Public Schools, 1864–1964," (Ph.D. dissertation, University of California, Berkeley, 1964), 303, 332–333; David B. Tyack, "Bureaucracy and the Common School: The Example of Portland, 1851–1913," *AQ,* XIX (Fall 1967), 483–487; Cubberly, *The Portland Survey,* 125–128; DeWeese, "Better School Administration," 64–66.

13. W. F. Phelps, "The Country School Problem," 8–9, 12–13; Olney, "The Country-School Problem," 36; *USAR* (1878/79), lxiii–lxv; *USAR* (1881/82), liv; *USAR* (1883/84), xxxi–xxxiv; *USAR* (1886/87), 173–176; Raab, "The Rural School Problem," 575; Emerson E. White, "The Country School Problem," *APNEA* (1894), 677–678; Lawton B. Evans, remarks, *APNEA* (1896), 271. On proposals for rural unification, see "Consolidation of Schools and Transportation of Students," *USAR* (1900/1901), I, 161–213; *USAR* (1894/95), II, 1469–1482; *USAR* (1895/96), II, 1353–1358; *USAR* (1898/99), I, 526–529; *USAR* (1899/1900), II, 2581–2584; *USAR* (1901/02), II, 2353–2369.

14. The organizational impulse also gave impetus to the movement to provide free standardized textbooks to students; see "Free Text-Books—Benefits, Objections, and Costs," *USAR* (1901/02), I, 632–640. Simultaneously, a nationally accepted understanding of the nature and purpose of education began to emerge; see Doty and Harris, *A Statement of the Theory of Education;* Münsterberg, *The Americans,* 365–366; "Report of the Committee on Interstate Recognition of High Grade Teachers' Certificates," *APNEA* (1905), 240; F. W. Hewes, "Common Schools of the United States," *HW,* XXXVII (February 10, 1894), 140; Sizer, *Secondary Schools,* 14–16.

15. *USAR* (1882/83), lxxxix.

16. Adams, "Scientific Common-School Education," *HM,* LXI (October 1880), 937; Maxwell, "City School Systems," *USAR* 1891/92), II, 666; *USAR* (1892/93), II, 1795; Haber, *Effi-*

ciency and Uplift, 64; Gove, "Limitations of the Superintendent's Authority," 152–157.

17. Draper, "Common Schools in Larger Cities," 391; Charles B. Gilbert, "The Freedom of the Teacher," *APNEA* (1903), 165–167; Greenwood, "Verbatim Reports of Recitations in Arithmetic in the Schools of Kansas City, Missouri," *USAR* 1893/94), I, 557 and *passim;* Charles D. Hine, "The Creation of an Education Machine," *USAR* (1893/94), II, 1360; Cubberly, *The Portland Survey,* 125; Tyack, *Turning Points,* 316; Cubberly, *Changing Conceptions,* 55–57.

18. Philbrick, *City School Systems,* 58; Tyack, *Turning Points,* 319.

19. Chamberlain, "Growth of the Power of the Superintendent," 248, 293–294.

20. Nicholas Murray Butler, "What Knowledge Is of the Most Worth?" *APNEA* (1895), 70.

21. Pickard, "City Systems of Management," 71–72; George H. Howison, "What the Public Schools Should Teach the American Laborer," *APNEA* (1888), 244–249; Committee on City School Systems, "School Superintendence in Cities," *APNEA* (1890), 309, 312–313; William H. Maxwell, "City School Systems," *APNEA* (1890), 447–448; *Report of the Committee of Fifteen,* 77; Jones, "The Politician and the Public School," 813; Hinsdale, "City School Systems," 251–252; Preston W. Search, *An Ideal School, or Looking Forward* (New York: Appleton, 1903), 13; "A Symposium on Herbert Spencer," *APNEA* (1905), 214–235; Butler, "Status of Education at the Close of the Century," *USAR* (1899/1900), I, 563, 567; Harris, "Does the Common School Educate Children above the Station They Are Expected to Occupy in Life?" *Education,* III (May 1883), 461–464; Harris, "City School Supervision–V," 168–169; Harris, "The Education of the Negro," *AM,* LXIX (June 1892), 721–722, 726; Harris, "Twenty Years' Progress in Education," *APNEA* (1892), 56–57; Harris, "The Educational Lessons of the Census," *APNEA* (1883), 29–32, 42; Merle Curti, *The Social Ideas of American Educators* (Totowa, N.J.: Littlefield, Adams, 1966), 310–347.

22. Harris, "Does the Common School Educate?" 461–462; Harris, "Educational Lessons of the Census," 35–36; Harris, "Twenty Years' Progress," 57; Curti, *Social Ideas,* 444; Maxwell, "Education for Efficiency," 63; N. Cropsey, "A Short Review of the Educational Progress of the Year," *APNEA* (1905), 373; Howe, *The City, The Hope of Democracy* (New York: Scribner's, 1906), 46.

23. Addams, "Foreign-Born Children," 111; Doty and Harris, *A Statement of the Theory of Education,* 12, 14.

24. F. W. Hewes, "The Public Schools of the United States," *HW,* XXXIX (October 26, 1895), 1017; A. T. Hadley, "How Can the Business Man of the Future Be Best Educated?" *USAR* (1899/1900), II, 1375; John B. Walker, "What Should Be the Education of the Business Man?" *APNEA* (1905), 675–678; Cropsey, "A Short Review," 378; Pickard, "City Systems of Management," 73; *Report of the Committee of Fifteen,* 77; Hinsdale, "City School Systems," 253; George H. Martin, "Comparison of Modern Business Methods with Educational Methods," *APNEA* (1905), 321–322; Chamberlain, "Growth of the Power of the Superintendent," 387–389.

25. Carroll G. Pearse, "Some Reminiscences of the Association Meeting of 1884," *APNEA* (1934), 249; William H. Maxwell, "The Superintendent as a Man of Affairs," *APNEA* (1904), 259–264; Chamberlain, "Growth of the Power of the Superintendent," 293.

CHAPTER FOUR

1. "The Reminiscences of Christopher A. Buckley," SF *Bulletin,* Jan. 27, 1919; *Report of the Committee of Fifteen,* 77; Welter, *Popular Education,* 67–82 and *passim;* Pickard, "City Systems of Management," 72.

2. The synthesis of pre-reform urban school organization is derived from sources cited herein.

3. William Marcy Tweed, James McManes of Philadelphia, and Abraham Ruef of San Francisco were all involved with city schools in early stages of their careers; see Harold Zink, *City Bosses in the United States: A Study of Twenty Municipal Bosses* (Durham, N.C. Duke University Press, 1931), 101, 196; Walton Bean, *Boss Ruef's San Francisco* (Berkeley, Calif.: University of California Press, 1952), chap. 1; Dolson, "Administration," 298.

    USAR (1876/77), ix; Howison, "What the Public Schools Should Teach," 249; Pickard, "City Systems of Management," 72; Maxwell, "City School Systems," *APNEA* (1890), 456–458; Rice, "A Plan to Free the Public Schools from Politics," 501; *Report of the Committee of Fifteen,* 81; Gove, "Limitations of the Superintendent's Authority," 154–156; F. Louis Soldan, "Charter Provisions as Related to the Reorganization of School Systems," *APNEA* (1905), 231–232; Cropsey, "A Short Review," 378; Cubberly, *Changing Conceptions,* 65.

4. "Confessions of Three School Superintendents," *AM,*

LXXXII (November 1898), 644–651; "Confessions of Public School Teachers," 101–102; Rice, "Evils in Baltimore," 152; Hall, "The Case of the Public Schools," 405; Jones, "The Politician and the Public School," 812–815; Ernst, "The Movement for School Reform in Boston," 439; Tyack, *Turning Points,* 417–418.

5. Gove, "Report of the Committee on City School Systems," 464; Philbrick, *City School Systems,* 15.

6. Cubberly, "The School Situation," 365–366; Dolson, "Administration," 139 ff.

7. Dolson, "Administration," 139, 209, 227, 230–234, 262–270; John Swett, *History of the Public School System of California* (San Francisco: Bancroft, 1876), 59, 77; John Swett, *Public Education in California* (New York: American Book, 1911), 114; California State Superintendent of Public Instruction, *Second Biennial Report* (San Francisco: n.p., 1867), 136–137.

8. SF *Evening Bulletin,* Nov. 28, 1878; SF *Chronicle,* Nov. 29, 1878; San Francisco Board of Education, *The School Scandal of San Francisco* (San Francisco: n.p., 1878), 5; California, *Constitution* (1879), Article X, Section 3; John W. Taylor, *Annual Report of the Superintendent of Schools of San Francisco* (San Francisco: n.p., 1880), 442.

9. Alexander B. Callow, Jr., "San Francisco's Blind Boss," *PHR,* XXV (August 1956), 261–265, 269. For Buckley's career after 1891, see William A. Bullough, "The Steam Beer Handicap: Chris Buckley and the San Francisco Municipal Election of 1896," forthcoming in *CHQ* See also Dolson, "Administration," 237–238.

10. SF *Chronicle,* Jan. 6, 1883; Jan. 12, 1883; Jan. 20, 1883; SF *Daily Examiner,* Jan. 11, 1883; SF *Call,* Jan. 13, 1883.

11. SF *Daily Examiner,* Jan. 14, 1885; Jan. 15, 1885; Jan. 18, 1885; Dolson, "Administration," 307; Jeremiah Lynch, *Buckleyism: The Government of a State* (San Francisco: n.p., 1889), 17; John Swett, *Annual Report of the Superintendent of Schools of San Francisco* (San Francisco: n.p., 1892), 146; Cubberly, "The School Situation," 370 – 371; SF *Chronicle,* Jan. 5, 1900.

   See Robert K. Merton, *Social Theory and Social Structure* (New York: Free Press, 1957), 71–81, for a perceptive analysis of the social implications of the political machine.

12. Frank W. Blackmar, "San Francisco's Struggle for Good Government," *Forum,* XXVI (January 1899), 569.

13. *Ibid.,* 566. See also A. Knapp, "San Francisco and the Civic Awakening," *Arena,* XII (April 1895), 241–249; James D.

Phelan, "Municipal Conditions in San Francisco," *Arena,* XVII (June 1897), 989–995; J. D. Phelan, "Municipal Conditions and the New Charter," *OM,* XXVII (July 1896), 104–111; Charter Convention of 100, *Reports of Committees* (San Francisco: n.p., 1897); Dolson, "Administration," 289–299, 364–366; Cubberly, "The School Situation," 372–373.

14. SF *Chronicle,* Jan. 1, 1900; Jan. 4, 1900; Jan. 9, 1900; Dolson, "Administration," 722, 725. The Charter of 1898 did not become effective until January 1, 1900.

15. Cubberly, "The School Situation," 373–375; Dolson, "Administration," 289–299, 332–333; SF *Chronicle,* Jan. 13, 1900; Jan. 20, 1900; Jan. 25, 1900; Jan. 30, 1900.
    On Ruef, see Bean, *Boss Ruef's San Francisco,* chaps. 1 and 2, and James P. Walsh, "Abe Ruef Was No Boss: Machine Politics, Reform, and San Francisco," *CHQ,* LI (Spring 1972), 3–16.

16. Cubberly, "The School Situation," 379–381.

17. *USAR* (1895/96), I, 15–18; Hammack, "Centralization," 1–2, 5–6, 12–19, 91–122, *passim;* Stewart, "Unsanitary Schools and Public Indifference," 109–110; Cohen, *Progressives and Urban School Reform,* 26–28; Nicholas Murray Butler, editorial, *ER,* XIV (September 1897), 207.

18. Katz, "The Emergence of Bureaucracy," 155–188, 319–357; Ernst, "School Reform in Boston," 433–441; Wetmore, "Boston School Administration," 105–110, 112–114, 117; Lazerson, *Origins of the Urban School,* 3–4; Adams, "Scientific Common School Education," 934–942.

19. Rice, "The Public School System of Philadelphia," 310–317; Shaw, "The Public Schools of a Boss-Ridden City," 4460–4466; Lincoln Steffens, *The Shame of the Cities* (New York: Hill & Wang, 1965 [1904]), 155; William H. Issel, "Modernization in Philadelphia School Reform, 1882–1905," *PMHB,* XCIV (July 1970), 358–373; Rice, "Evils in Baltimore," 156–157; Boykin, "Organization of City School Boards," 246; *USAR* (1895/96), I, 74; Brown and others, *Report of the Commission,* 29–33; Strayer, "The Baltimore School Situation," 327–345.

20. Counts, *School and Society in Chicago,* 18–32; Nicholas Murray Butler, editorial, *ER,* XIV (October 1897), 309–311; DeWeese, "Better School Administration," 61–63; Eliot, "A Nonpartisan School Law," 224–226; Greenwood, "School Reminiscences," 346–348; Jones, "The Politician and the Public School," 815–822; Boykin, "Organization of City School Boards," 238–239; Cubberly, *The Portland Survey,*

125–128; Tyack, "Bureaucracy and the Common School," 478–490; David B. Tyack, "City Schools: Centralization of Control at the Turn of the Century," in Jerry Israel (ed.), *Building the Organizational Society: Essays on Associational Activities in Modern America* (New York: Free Press, 1972), 57–72; McKelvey, *Rochester,* 32–39, 104.

21. Samuel P. Hays, "The Politics of Reform in Municipal Government in the Progressive Era," *PNQ,* LV (October 1964), 157–169; James Weinstein, "Organized Business and the City Commission and Manager Movements," *JSH,* XXVIII (May 1962), 167–181; Eric L. McKitrick, "The Study of Corruption," *PSQ,* LXXII (December 1957), 502–514; Richard Hofstadter, *The Age of Reform* (New York: Vintage, 1955), 131 ff; Howe, "The Big Red Schoolhouse," 267; Hinsdale, "City School Systems," 252; Rice, "A Plan to Free the Schools from Politics," 500; Draper, "Common Schools," 396; *Report of the Committee of Fifteen,* 80–81.

22. *The Nation,* XVIII (April 9, 1874), 231; *USAR* (1879/79), vii; Draper, "Common Schools," 396–397; Jones, "The Politician and the Public School, 813; Rice, "A Plan to Free the Schools from Politics," 500–501; *Report of the Committee of Fifteen,* 132; Cubberly, *Changing Conceptions,* 65.

23. Draper, "Plans of Organization," 299, 307.

24. For a lucid analysis of distinctions between structural and social or functional reform, see Melvin G. Holli, *Reform in Detroit: Hazen S. Pingree and Urban Politics* (New York: Oxford University Press, 1969), 157–181.

25. "Martin Kelly's Story," SF *Bulletin,* Nov. 16, 1917.

CHAPTER FIVE

1. David Donald, *Lincoln Reconsidered* (New York: Knopf, 1956), 21–36; Hofstadter, *Age of Reform,* 131–173; Robert A. Skotheim, "A Note on Historical Method: David Donald's 'Toward a Reconsideration of Abolitionists,' " *JSH,* XXV (August 1959), 356–365; Martin B. Duberman, "The Abolitionists and Psychology," *JNH,* XLVII (July 1962), 183–192.

2. *National Cyclopaedia of American Biography,* V, 553; VI, 421; X, 44, 471; XII, 203, 218, 498, 510, 516, 531; XIII, 62, 203; XV, 1; XXI, 62; XXX, 12; XXXIX, 469; *Who Was Who in America,* I, 125; IV, 196.

3. Hays, "The Politics of Reform," 169.

4. Maxwell, "City School Systems," 449, 460; Butler, "What Knowledge Is of the Most Worth?" 69–80.

5. On education as social control, see David B. Tyack, "Education and Social Unrest, 1873–1878," *HER*, XXI (Spring 1961), 194–212; Wiebe, "The Social Functions of Public Education," 147–164; White, "Education in the Turn-of-the-Century City," 169–182; Lazerson, *Origins of Urban Education*, chap. 4; Katz, *Class, Bureaucracy, and Schools*, 52–55; Butler, "What Knowledge Is of the Most Worth?" 70–77; Butler, "The Status of Education," 563–571; Snyder, "Education for the Industrial Classes," 761–763; Harris, "Does the Common School Educate?" 461–475; Pickard, "City Systems of Management," 69; Howison, "What the Common Schools Should Teach," 243–249; W. R. Garrett, "The Limits of Education," *APNEA* (1877), 33–39; William T. Harris, "Statistics versus Socialism," *Forum*, XXIV (October 1897), 186–199; *USAR* (1891/92), II, 662; George H. Martin, "New Standards of Patriotic Citizenship," *APNEA* (1895), 137.

6. Pickard, "City Systems of Management," 70–75; J. P. Irish, "The Schools Fail to Give a Proper Preparation for Active Life," *APNEA* (1888), 151–155; S. F. Scovel, "In Fundamental, What Shall We Teach as the American Doctrine of Church and State?" *APNEA* (1899), 616–624; Francis Bellamy, "Americanism in the Public Schools," *APNEA* (1892), 61–67; Martin, "New Standards of Patriotic Citizenship," 134–135; Search, *An Ideal School*, 13, 315; Cropsey, "A Short Review," 376.

7. Curti, *Social Ideas*, 313–315; David Shannon (ed.), *Beatrice Webb's American Diary* (Madison, Wisc.; University of Wisconsin Press, 1963), 37; Harris, "The Education of the Negro," 722, 725; Harris, "Educational Lessons of the Census," 31, 36; Harris, "Statistics versus Socialism," 186–199.

8. Harris, "Twenty Years' Progress," 56; Harris, "The Present Status of Education in the United States," *APNEA* (1891), 140; Harris, "Is There Enough Work for All?" *Forum*, XXV (April 1898), 224–236; Harris, "Henry George's Mistake about Land," *Forum*, III (July 1887), 434–442; John S. Roberts, *William T. Harris: A Critical Study of His Educational and Related Philosophical Views* (Washington, D.C.: NEA, 1924).

9. Parker, "Art in Everything," *APNEA* (1900), 513; Sizer, *Secondary Schools*, 14.

10. A. D. Mayo, "Education for Citizenship," *APNEA* (1887), 279; William E. Sheldon, "The Schools Fail to Give a Proper Preparation for Active Life," *APNEA* (1888), 148–149; *USAR* (1877/78), viii; *USAR* (1879/79), vii; Martin, "New Standards of Patriotic Citizenship," 137; Bellamy, "Ameri-

canism in Public Schools," 65–66; Parker, "Art in Everything," 511.

11. Morris I. Berger, "The Settlement, the Immigrant, and the Public School: A Study of the Influence of the Settlement Movement and the New Migration upon Public Education, 1890–1924," (Ph.D. dissertation, Columbia University, 1956), 25, 108. Educators frequently ignored the fact that many immigrants held similar goals for their own children, expected education to facilitate their achievement, and even sent their children to school in greater proportion than did native parents; see Timothy L. Smith, "Immigrant Social Aspirations and American Education, 1880–1930," *AQ*, XXI (Fall 1969), 523–527.

   USAR (1881/82), I, xlii–xliii; Maxwell, "Education for Efficiency," 62; Shaw, "The True Character of New York Public Schools," 4205; Thomas Hampson, "The Apprenticeship Question," *APNEA* (1885), 151; Irish, "The Schools Fail to Give a Proper Preparation," 146; Snyder, "Education for the Industrial Classes," 760; Cubberly, *Changing Conceptions,* 113; Luigi Bodio, "The Protection of Italian Immigrants in America," *USAR* (1894/95), II, 1789–1793; Stevens, "Child Slavery in America," 129; Addams, "Foreign-Born Children," 105–106.

12. Julia Richman, "The Immigrant Child," *APNEA* (1905), 117; A. R. Dugmore, "New Citizens for the Republic," *WW,* VII (April 1903), 3323–3326; J. R. Preston, remarks, *APNEA* (1891), 102–105, 115; Shaw, "The True Character of New York Public Schools," 4206.

13. Cubberly, *Changing Conceptions,* 15–16.

14. For analyses of reform "machines" as agencies of control, see John G. Sproat, *The Best Men: Liberal Reform in the Gilded Age* (New York: Oxford University Press, 1968), 256, and Holli, *Reform in Detroit,* 152–156.

15. In a recent study of political Progressives, Otis L. Graham found only three active educational leaders: Felix Adler, Nicholas Murray Butler, and John Dewey. See Graham, *An Encore for Reform* (New York: Oxford University Press, 1967). See also Eric F. Goldman, *Rendezvous with Destiny: A History of Modern American Reform* (New York: Vintage, 1956), 73 ff.; Welter, *Popular Education,* and Perkinson, *Imperfect Panacea.*

   Parker, "The School of the Future," 84. Despite abundant optimism, it should be noted, Parker was a strenuous advocate of the social function of public education.

16. Edward Atkinson, "Elementary Instruction in Mechanic Arts," *SM,* XXI (April 1881), 909; Philbrick, *City School*

Systems, 5; C. J. Baxter, "The Township High School," *APNEA* (1898), 310–311; Maxwell, "Education for Efficiency," 63; Cropsey, "A Short Review," 374–380; Rice, "Evils in Baltimore," 156; Rice, "The Public Schools of Boston," 767; Rice, "Schools of Buffalo and Cincinnati," 304; *USAR* (1877/78), vii; Shaw, "How Successful Are the Public Schools?" 5483; Canby, *The Age of Confidence,* 115.

17. See especially Harris's articles "The Educational Lessons of the Census," "The Present Status of Education," "Twenty Years' Progress," "Does the Common School Educate?" and "Is There Enough Work for All?"

18. "Child Study," *USAR* (1892/93), I, 357–391; Arthur MacDonald, "Child-Study in the United States," *USAR* (1897/98), II, 1281–1350; G. Stanley Hall, "New Departures in Education," *NAR,* CXL (February 1885), 144 – 152; G. S. Hall, "The New Psychology as a Basis for Education," *Forum,* XVIII (August 1894), 710–720; Welford Addis, "The Bertillon System as a Means for Suppressing the Business of Living by Crime," *USAR* (1895/96), II, 1299–1311; Charles Booth, "Social Pathology and Education," *USAR* (1889/90), I, 573–590; T. O. Crawford, "The Educational Power and Utility of Industrial Training and of Manual Training in Our Schools," *APNEA* (1888), 570–582; Adams, "Scientific School Education," 934–936; Cubberly, *Changing Conceptions,* 5.

19. See, for example, Arthur Mann, *Yankee Reformers in an Urban Age: Social Reform in Boston,* 1880–1900 (Cambridge, Mass.: Harvard University Press, 1954); Robert L. Beisner, *Twelve Against Empire: The Anti-Imperialists, 1898–1900* (New York: McGraw-Hill, 1968); Roy Lubove, *The Professional Altruist: The Emergence of Social Work as a Career* (Cambridge, Mass.: Harvard University Press, 1965), and Sproat, *The Best Men,* especially 247–248, which argues that liberal reformers became disillusioned with the business community, an attitude that educators did not share.

20. Sproat, *The Best Men,* 245, and chaps. 3 and 8.

21. Hinsdale, "City School Systems," 251, italics added; Maxwell, "Charter Provisions as Related to the Organization of School Systems," 220; Draper, "Common Schools," 394; *USAR* (1889/90), I, 573–590; Soldan, "Charter Provisions as Related to the Reorganization of School Systems," 231; Eliot, "A Nonpartisan School Law," 229; Cubberly, "The School Situation," 366; Shaw, "The Public Schools of a Boss-Ridden City," 4461–4463; "Confessions of Three Superintendents," 645; Sproat, *The Best Men,* 152; Warner, *The Urban Wilderness,* chaps. 2 and 6.

22. Sproat, *The Best Men,* 68; Harris, "The Education of the

Negro," 722; Hammack, "Centralization," 17; F. W. Hewes, "Common Schools of the United States," *HW*, XXXVII (February 10, 1894), 139; *USAR* (1883/84), cxx; *USAR* (1882/83), lxxvii; Winthrop Talbot, "A Public School in the Slums That Does Its Job," *WW*, XVIII (May 1909), 11567–11572; Frances E. Willard, "The White Cross Movement in Education," *APNEA* (1890), 159–178; Shaw, "How Successful Are the Public Schools?" 5482; *USAR* (1897/98), I, 869–871; Nicholas Murray Butler, "The Reform in Secondary Education in the United States," *USAR* (1892/93), II, 1453; William T. Harris, "The Curriculum for Secondary Schools," *USAR* (1892/93), II, 1462; Charles W. Eliot, "The Unity of Educational Reform," *USAR* (1892/93), II, 1472–73.

23. M. A. Newell, "President's Address," *APNEA* (1877), 6, 12–13; J. P. Wickersham, "Education and Crime,"*APNEA* (1881), 55; *USAR* (1883/84), lxxxvi; L. H. Jones, "The School and the Criminal," *APNEA* (1892), 209, 211; Scovel, "In Fundamental, What Shall We Teach?" 621; Maxwell, "Education for Efficiency," 61.

24. Wiebe, "The Social Functions of Public Education," 150; italics added.

25. Howe, *The City*, 33.

CHAPTER SIX

Chapter Six appeared in somewhat different form in *The Historian*, XXXV (February 1973), 183–195.

1. Schlesinger, *The Rise of the City*, 1878–1898 (New York: Harper, 1933), chap. 3.

2. For interesting and stimulating analyses of this aspect of American thought, see Leo Marx, *The Machine in the Garden: Technology and the Pastoral Ideal in America* (New York: Oxford University Press, 1964); Peter J. Schmitt, *Back to Nature: The Arcadian Myth in Urban America* (New York: Oxford University Press, 1969); Morton and Lucia White, *The Intellectual versus the City: From Thomas Jefferson to Frank Lloyd Wright* (Cambridge, Mass: Harvard University Press, 1962); Anselm Strauss, *Images of the American City* (New York: Free Press, 1961), 167–198; Canby, *The Age of Confidence*, 216.

3. Howe, *The City*, 301; Harris, "Twenty Years' Progress," 57; Harris, "The Education of the Negro," 726.

4. Evans, remarks, *APNEA* (1896), 270.

5. Martin G. Brumbaugh, "The Function of Nature in Elemen-

tary Education," *APNEA* (1896), 146; Spalding, "The Teacher and the School," *APNEA* (1896), italics added.

6. Hall, "The Story of a Sand-Pile," *SM,* III (July 1888), 696; Parker, "The Farm as the Center of Interest," *APNEA* (1897), 527–536; Cremin, *Transformation of the School,* 129.

7. Ellise B. Payne, "The Problems of the City Kindergarten Movement," *APNEA* (1896), 510; Hall, remarks, *APNEA* (1896), 158; Jordan, "Nature Study and Moral Culture," *APNEA* (1896), 130.

8. Search, *An Ideal School,* 104 and *passim.* See also Search, "Individualism in Mass Education," *APNEA* (1895), 398–406.

9. Nash, *Wilderness and the American Mind* (New Haven, Conn.: Yale University Press, 1967), chap. 9; Howe, *The City,* 33; Canby, *The Age of Confidence,* 214.

10. Butler, "What Knowledge Is of the Most Worth?" 76; Schmitt, *Back to Nature,* chap. 7; Mary R. Alling, "Natural Science in the Common Schools," *Education,* I (July 1881), 601–615; Oliver S. Wescott, "Nature Study," *APNEA* (1896), 139–141; Evangeline Whitney, "Nature Study as an Aid to Advanced Work in Science," *APNEA* (1904), 889–896.

Concern for rural schools parallels interest in nature study. See, for example, Phelps, "The Country School Problem," 7–15; Olney, "The Country-School Problem," 30–39; White, "The Country School Problem," 669–678; Raab, "The Rural School Problem," 571–578. Problems included economic distress, cultural decline, lack of qualified teachers, poor attendance, and public apathy. However, the exodus of rural populations to urban centers and the declining importance of the farm in American life remained the central concerns. These same concerns prompted Theodore Roosevelt's formation of the Commission on Country Life; see its *Report,* U.S. Senate Document 705, 60th Cong. 2d Sess. (1909).

11. *USAR* (1887/88), 159–160; "School Gardens," *USAR* (1898/99), I, 1082–1084; Rice "The Public Schools of Minneapolis and Others," *Forum,* XV (May 1893), 376.

12. Henry S. Curtis, "Vacation Schools, Playgrounds, and Settlements," *USAR* (1902/03), I, 2–7; Evangeline Whitney, "Vacation Schools, Playgrounds, and Recreation Centers," *APNEA* (1904), 298–303.

13. Canby, *The Age of Confidence,* 223; Maxwell, "The Grammar School Curriculum," 478.

14. Hall, "The Content of Children's Minds on Entering School," *PS,* I (June 1891), 155–156; Canby, *The Age of Confidence,* 116.

15. *USAR* (1876/77), vii; *USAR* (1877/78), vii–viii; Maurice Kirby, "The Study of Social Economy in Public Schools," *APNEA* (1877), 82–93 and *passim*.

16. For general treatments of the movement, see Melvin M. Barlow, *History of Industrial Education in the United States* (Peoria, Ill.: Charles A. Bennett, 1967), chap. 2; Charles A. Bennett, *History of Manual and Industrial Education* (Peoria, Ill.: Manual Arts Press, 1937), 313–321; Anderson, *History of Manual and Industrial School Education,* 156–165. For a lively analysis of the ideologies involved, see Berenice N. Fisher, *Industrial Education: American Ideals and Institutions* (Madison, Wisc.: University of Wisconsin, 1967).

17. Woodward, "Manual Training," *APNEA* (1883), 84–99; Woodward, *The Manual Training School* (Boston: Heath, 1887); Woodward, "The Result of the St. Louis Manual Training School," *APNEA* (1889), 73–91; "Report on the Experiment in Industrial Education in Boston," *APNEA* (1883), 17–20; Judson E. Hoyt, "Manual Training in the Public Schools of Smaller Cities," *APNEA* (1896), 768–777; Annette Johnson, "The Manual Training System of Los Angeles," *APNEA* (1899), 928–931; Paul Hoffman, "Manual Training in New York City Schools," *APNEA* (1892), 471–474; Charles A. Bennett, "Manual Training from the Kindergarten to High School," *APNEA* (1892), 449; Nicholas Murray Butler, "A Conference on Manual Training," *ER,* II (December 1891), 503–504; Calvin M. Woodward, "New Demands upon Schools by the World's Industries," *APNEA* (1893), 594–597.

18. Alexander Hogg, "Industrial Education, or the Equal Cultivation of the Head, the Heart, and the Hand," *APNEA* (1879), 74; Felix Adler, "Technical and Art Education in the Schools as Elements of Culture," *APNEA* (1884), 308–309; Charles A. Bennett, "The Aesthetic Principle in Manual Training," *APNEA* (1896), 786–790; C. F. Carroll, "Manual Training and the Course of Study," *APNEA* (1896), 778–786; Flora J. White, "The Physical Effects of Sloyd," *APNEA* (1896), 766; J. A. Addicott, "Correlation of Manual Training with other Branches of Study," *APNEA* (1899), 923–928; Vinton S. Paessler, "The Educational Value of Metal Working," *APNEA* (1899), 915; Howison, "What the Public Schools Should Teach," 246; W. N. Ackley, "The True Idea of American Labor," *APNEA* (1888), 240; Lazerson, *Origins of the Urban School,* 97–100; Nellie S. Kedzie, "The Need for Manual Training for Girls," *APNEA* (1896), 756; H. M. Leipziger, "Education as Affected by Manual Training," *APNEA* (1892), 439–443; Albert E. Robinson, "Industrial Education a Necessity of the Times," *APNEA* (1895), 743;

J. R. Buchanan, "The Moral Influence of Manual Training," *APNEA* (1883), 46.

19. William T. Harris, "What Shall the Public Schools Teach?" *Forum,* IV (February 1888), 573–581; W. T. Harris, "Industrial Education in the Common Schools," *Education,* V (June 1886), 605–611; George T. Fairchild, "Some Limitations on Industrial Training," *APNEA* (1888), 549; James N. Greenwood, "Where Should General Education End and Special Education Begin?" *APNEA* (1888), 182–192; R. K. Buehrle, "The Popular View: Education as Preparation to Earn a Living," *APNEA* (1888), 173–182; Harris, "The Educational Lessons of the Census," 33; L. S. Thompson, "Educated Labor," *APNEA* (1879), 203–208; L. S. Thompson, "The Decay of Apprenticeship: Its Cause and Remedies," *APNEA* (1881), 246–251; Hampson, "The Apprenticeship Question," 151–159; Snyder, "Education for the Industrial Classes," 758–763; Woodward, "Manual Training," 96–99.

20. Zalmon Richards, "The Relation of Industrial to Intellectual Training in Our Public Schools," *APNEA* (1888), 563–569; Robinson, "Industrial Education a Necessity of the Times," 742; Walker, "Manual Training in Urban Communities," *APNEA* (1887), 196; Woodward, *The Manual Training School;* Woodward, "The Function of the Public School," *APNEA* (1887), 212–224.

21. Surveys of nineteenth-century school books tend to support this assumption; see Ruth M. Elson, "American Schoolbooks and 'Culture' in the Nineteenth Century," *MVHR,* XLVI (December 1959), 411 – 434, and R. M. Elson, *Guardians of Tradition: American Schoolbooks of the Nineteenth Century* (Lincoln, Neb.: University of Nebraska Press, 1964).

    Gilbert, "Freedom of the Teacher," 165; Nash, *Wilderness and the American Mind,* 157.

22. DeGarmo, "Concentration of Studies as a Means of Developing Character," *APNEA* (1896), 311–312.

23. Maxwell, "City School Systems," 449.

24. See, for example, B. J. Chandler and others (eds.), *Education in Urban Society* (New York: Dodd-Mead, 1962), 3–4; and Bayles and Hood, *Growth of American Educational Thought and Practice,* 116.

CHAPTER SEVEN

1. Aspects of the functioning of public welfare services, from early poor laws through recent efforts to retrain and employ

relief recipients, also manifest the notions of compensatory education and control; see Frances Fox Piven and Richard A. Cloward, *Regulating the Poor: The Function of Public Welfare* (New York: Vintage, 1972), especially 3–38, 80–111, 200–256.

2. See documents in Tyack, *Turning Points,* 15–17, 35–49, 73, 86–89, 100, 102.

3. Mann, *Life and Works,* IV (Boston: Walker and Fuller, 1865–1868), 365; John R. Commons and others (eds.), *A History of Industrial Society,* V (Cleveland: Arthur H. Clark, 1910), 94–103, 195–199; Roy P. Baler (ed.), *The Collected Works of Abraham Lincoln,* I (New Brunswick, N.J.: Rutgers University Press, 1953), 8; *ibid.,* III, 481.

4. Welter, *Popular Education,* 141–150; Curti, *Social Ideas,* 261–287; Perkinson, *Imperfect Panacea,* 13–51; Henry Bullock, *History of Negro Education in the South from 1619 to the Present* (Cambridge, Mass.: Harvard University Press, 1967), 17–32, 37–49; Henry L. Swint, *The Northern Teacher in the South, 1862–1870* (New York: Octagon, 1967), 23–76.

5. The Blair Bill never passed the House of Representatives and finally died in the Senate in 1890; see U.S., *Congressional Record,* 48th Cong. 2nd Sess. (March 18, 1884), 1999; U.S., *Congressional Record,* 46th Cong. 3rd Sess. (December 15, 1880), 148–149; Atticus G. Haygood, "If Universal Suffrage, Then Universal Education," *APNEA* (1883), 43–54; A. A. Gunby, "The Race Problem," *APNEA* (1890), 254–266; Hogg, "The Problem of the Hour," 299–300; Curti, *Social Ideas,* 264–266, 271.

6. Richman, "The Immigrant Child," 116; Maxwell, "Education for Efficiency," 65; Draper, "Common Schools in Larger Cities," 385–386; Richard Watson Gilder, "The New York Kindergarten Association," *ER,* I (January 1891), 59–60; Caroline T. Haven, "The Relation of the Kindergarten to Manual Training," *APNEA* (1892), 447; *USAR* (1881/82), cxxxvii; *USAR* (1882/83), cvi–cvix.

7. Katz, *Class, Bureaucracy, and Schools,* subtitle.

8. Cohen, *Progressives and Urban School Reform,* 26–29; Hammack, "Centralization," 15–18, 23; Lubove, *The Professional Altruist,* 14.

9. Woods, *The City Wilderness,* 49, 103–106, 118, 123–124, 232–238; Riis, "The Children of the Poor," 549–550; Josephine Shaw Lowell, "Methods of Relief for the Unemployed," *Forum,* XVI (February 1894), 658; Riis, *The Battle with the Slum,* 185–186; Addams, "Foreign-Born Children," 105–106;

Howe, "Settlers in the City Wilderness," 18–23; Lubove, *The Professional Altruist,* chaps. 1 and 2.

10. *USAR* (1896/97), I, 623–629; Shaw, "The True Character of New York Public Schools," 4206–4207; Horace E. Scudder, "The School-house as a Centre," *AM,* LXXVII (January 1896), 107–109, Riis; *The Battle with the Slum,* 402–403.

11. Berger, "The Settlement, the Immigrant, and the Public School," 16 – 19. Though Berger finds the kindergarten relatively unimportant in public education until the twentieth century, statistics indicate that by 1902 there were 3,244 public kindergartens enrolling 205,432 pupils and employing 5,935 teachers, nearly all in cities; see *USAR* (1901/02), II, 2273.

    Stickney, "The Homes of Our Down-Town Children," 392; Gilder, "The New York Kindergarten Association," 60.

12. Mary E. McDowell, "The Children of Our Cities," *APNEA* (1896), 491; Amalie Hofer, "The Social Settlement and the Kindergarten," *APNEA* (1895), 520–525; Wilhelmina Caldwell, "Mother's Meetings—How to Conduct Them among the Poor," *APNEA* (1895), 535–538; Evans, "The Factory Child," 246; Jane Addams, "Child Labor," *APNEA* (1905), 260; Wickersham, "Education and Crime," 45–55; Jones, "The School and the Criminal," 208–217; Willard, "The White Cross Movement," 159–165; Haven, "The Relation of the Kindergarten to Manual Training," 444–448; Emma Marwedel, "Prevention of Criminal Idleness," *APNEA* (1893), 372–381.

13. Hall, "New Departures in Education," 144–152; Hall, "The New Psychology as a Basis for Education," 710–720; Parker, "The Work of the Illinois Society for Child Study," *APNEA* (1896), 844–846.

    For a brief analysis of Dewey's concept of urban education, see Oscar Handlin, *John Dewey's Challenge to Education: Historical Perspectives on the Cultural Context* (New York: Harper's, 1959), chaps. 1 and 2.

14. Davidson, *The Education of the Wage Earners,* comp. Charles M. Bakewell (Boston: Ginn, 1904), 1–6, 10–12, 44, 47–52, 96–101, 229–233.

    Davidson was perhaps unique among intellectuals of his era, for he exhibited none of the condescension or paternalism common among others in their dealings with immigrants.

15. *Ibid.,* 123, 216–227.

16. Patri, *A Schoolmaster of the Great City* (New York: Macmillan, 1917), 3–5, 14–18, 50–57, 77–84, 114, 197–219.

17. Evidence does not permit an unequivocal assessment of teacher

attitudes. However, if the observations of critics and the admissions of administrators are considered, the apparent conclusion is that most teachers in urban schools had little real empathy with their students or genuine concern for them. Rice, "The Public Schools of Boston," 765; Rice, "The Public Schools of St. Louis and Indianapolis," 443; *USAR* (1882/83), lxxxv–lxxxvi; Shaw, "The Public Schools of a Boss-Ridden City," 4461; Shaw, "The True Character of New York Public Schools," 4206–4207; William H. Maxwell, "Stories of the Lives of Real Teachers," *WW*, XVIII (August 1909), 11877–11880; Talbot, "A Public School in the Slums that Does Its Job," 11567–11570; Jones, "Report of the Committee on Public School Systems," 277; Adele M. Shaw, "First-Hand Education in Sensible Schools," *WW*, VIII (July 1904), 4996–5004.

CHAPTER EIGHT

1. Cremin, *Transformation of the School.*

2. *USAR* (1881/82), cvii.

3. Current discussions of urban educational problems continue to presume that difficulties in city schools are related almost exclusively to poverty, political impotence, and ethnic imbalance. It should be understood also that even in white middle-class urban communities, school problems differ from those of the inner city only in degree. See William M. Perel and Philip D. Vairo, *Urban Education: Problems and Prospects* (New York: David McKay, 1969), 42; Peter Schrag, *Village School Downtown: Politics and Education—A Boston Report* (Boston: Beacon, 1967), 160–161; Matthew J. Pillard, "Teachers for Urban Schools," in Chandler and others, *Education in Urban Society,* 193–210; Robert J. Havighurst, *The Public Schools of Chicago* (Chicago: Board of Education, 1964), 175; Roald F. Campbell and others, *Education and Urban Renaissance* (New York: Wiley, 1969), 9; Norton E. Long, "Education and Metropolitan Change," in Chandler and others, *Education in Urban Society,* 84–88.

Numerous pedagogical expatriates from the city have recorded their experiences with the school bureaucracy; see Bel Kaufman, *Up the Down Staircase* (New York: Prentice-Hall, 1964); Herbert R. Kohl, *36 Children* (New York: New American Library, 1967); Jonathan Kozol, *Death at an Early Age* (Boston: Houghton Mifflin, 1967), and James Herndon, *The Way It Spozed to Be* (New York: Simon & Schuster, 1968).

4. Cubberly, *The Portland Survey,* 32.

5. David B. Tyack, "Needed—A Reform of a Reform," subsequently published as "City Schools: Centralization of Control at the Turn of the Century," in Israel, *Building the Organizational Society,* 57–72; Perel and Vairo, *Urban Education,* 58–59; Katz, *Class, Bureaucracy, and Schools,* chap. 3; Ronald and Beatrice Gross (eds.), *Radical School Reform* (New York: Simon & Schuster, 1970), 60 – 61, 67.

6. Morris Janowitz, *Institution Building in Urban Education* (Hartford: Russell Sage Foundation, 1969), 68–69, 100–102; Perel and Vairo, *Urban Education,* 127–128; Mario Fantini and Gerald Weinstein, *Making Urban Schools Work* (New York: Holt, Rinehart and Winston, 1968), 53–60; John W. Polley, "Decentralization in Urban School Systems," in Chandler and others, *Education in Urban Society,* 117–118; McGeorge Bundy, *Reconnection for Learning: A Community School System for New York City* (New York: n.p., 1967).

7. Campbell and others, *Education and Urban Renaissance,* 11–12; Fantini and Weinstein, *Making Urban Schools Work,* 5–11; Schrag, *Village School Downtown,* 159–161; Janowitz, *Institution Building,* 16, 23–24; Aaron V. Cicourel, "Administrative Science and Education in Urban Society," in Chandler and others, *Education in Urban Society,* 143–146.

8. Janowitz, *Institution Building,* 23–24; Schrag, *Village School Downtown,* 163, 165–167.

9. Parker, "The School of the Future," 86; Perel and Vairo, *Urban Education,* 4–7, 95–99; Schrag, *Village School Downtown,* 156.
   One example of middle-class "backlash" is the 1965 election of Louise Day Hicks to the Boston School Committee following a campaign that began with opposition to busing to achieve racial balance and ultimately involved nearly every aspect of urban school management; see Schrag, *Village School Downtown.*

10. Janowitz, *Institution Building,* 17, 20–23.
   In response to demands for "clearly discernible results," in July of 1970 Governor Ronald Reagan of California signed into law the "Ryan Act" (Teacher Preparation and Licensing Law of 1970, AB 122), which provides for teacher training, certification, and evaluation based upon specific "competencies." The statute illustrates continuing commitment to educational reform through institutional manipulation.

11. Perel and Vairo, *Urban Education,* 19; Schrag, *Village School Downtown,* 155; B. J. Chandler, "Forces Influencing Urban Schools," in Chandler and others, *Education in Urban Society,* 5–10.

12. Absence of full understanding remains. In a conversation with a former OEO official, it was learned that San Diego, California, Mexican-American youths are being taught automobile upholstering. In Tijuana, Mexico, a few miles across the border, an automobile can be completely reupholstered for less than half American prices, and Californians have traditionally visited the Mexican city for that express purpose. Thus the San Diego market for skilled upholsterers is limited, and the decision to train local youth in that skill reflects limited understanding of community realities.

13. Perel and Vairo, *Urban Education,* 26–27, 31–33, 36–37; Campbell and others, *Education and Urban Renaissance,* 9–10; Kenneth B. Clark, *Dark Ghetto* (New York: Harper & Row, 1965), 128–129.

14. DeGarmo, "Concentration of Studies as a Means of Developing Character," 315.

15. Cropsey, "A Short Review," 379.

16. In neither city planning nor education has the commitment to nature reached its demise. The weakness lies not in the notion that parks and recreation facilities are inherently beneficial, but rather in the assumption that nature, once established in the city, will take its course to solve urban problems. See Jane Jacobs, *The Death and Life of Great American Cities* (New York: Modern Library, 1969), 3–28; Bayles and Hood, *The Growth of American Educational Thought and Practice,* 116–117; Chandler and others, *Education in Urban Society,* 3–4; Benjamin C. Willis, "The Quest for Quality Education in a Major City," in Chandler and others, *Education in Urban Society,* 230–231; David Lewis, "Great High Schools, Their Impact on Model Cities Neighborhoods: The Pittsburgh Plan," in Campbell and others, *Education and Urban Renaissance,* 73–92. Paul T. Ringenbach, "Discarding Rural Nostrums for City Problems: Moving Toward Urban Reform," *RMSSJ,* X (January 1973), 33–42, argues that intellectual agrarianism is no longer a significant factor.

17. Curti, *Social Ideas,* 581.

18. Some of the ideas expressed have been revived and refurbished. The Federal Model Cities Act of 1966, for example, makes the school the central agency for community co-ordination in much the same manner envisioned by late nineteenth-century settlement workers. See Janowitz, *Institution Building,* 110–114; Campbell and others, *Education for Urban Renaissance,* 136–140 and *passim.*

A Note on Sources

The published documentary material relating to all phases of the history of education in the United States is voluminous, varied, and readily accessible to interested scholars. Because a major objective of the present study involves a critical comparative assessment of the rhetoric and practice of educational reform in Gilded Age cities, it is based almost entirely upon such sources. Indeed, the bulk of the data here used results from a comprehensive survey of thirty years' output of just two major educational records, *Annual Reports* and other publications of the U.S. Bureau of Education and the yearly *Journals of Addresses and Proceedings* of the National Education Association. These sources must be approached with caution because they reflect essentially the perspective of the professional hierarchy. However, understanding precisely that point of view is essential to the analysis of educational reform. Comparing what educators said and wrote with what they did reveals that, in most cases, they were quite candid.

Each of the major sources also provides important insights for understanding the intellectual climate of the late nineteenth century as it applied to cities and schools. *Annual Reports* record the "official" or government position, and special Bureau of Education publications, including periodic Bulletins and Circulars of Information, supplement the record with analyses of specific programs, events, or problems. Among these, John D. Philbrick's *City School Systems of the United States,* written by the bureau's expert on urban education, is especially useful. The NEA *Proceedings,* on the other hand, record events and discussions at each annual association convention, making their value apparent. They

177

have the added utility of documenting not only the ideas of eminent members of the profession but also the responses and opinions of their colleagues, thereby preserving elements of the pedagogical debate and dialogue of the period. For any scholar concerned with the multifaceted history of education in the United States, these two sources, by no means exhausted here, are a mine of important information and statistical data.

Contemporary journals are helpful supplementary sources for understanding the climate of ideas molding public education in American cities. The usefulness of professional journals such as *Educational Review, Education,* and *Pedagogical Seminary* is apparent, and such lay journals as *The Forum, Atlantic Monthly, World's Work,* and their numerous companions are equally important. Their pages provided a platform from which articulate urban educators expressed their ideas and discussed their programs and a forum for lay and professional critics. The sheer volume of published articles dealing explicitly with urban schools suggests a high degree of public interest.

Although not cited extensively in this study, state and local sources are available to document developments in specific cities and assess their relationships to national patterns. In virtually every city, school boards and superintendents published yearly reports, census data, and other documents, often under the specific mandate of city charters. These may be augmented with city council and similar records and with local newspapers which, used with caution, provide important perspectives on the development of urban school systems.

Secondary historical literature on the history of urban education is neither abundant nor particularly helpful; it adheres principally to a laudatory, uncritical approach reflecting the ideologies of educators themselves. Recently, however, scholars have broken with that tradition and are producing significant and incisive critical analyses of American educational thought and practice. Among them are historians David C. Hammack, Michael B. Katz, Marvin Lazerson, Stanley K. Schultz, David B. Tyack, and Robert Wiebe. In addition, scholars too numerous to mention, working on related problems in urban history, are providing tangential but significant insights into the evolution of urban school systems. Educators themselves have begun a critical reassessment of current problems, often with specific reference to the historical dimension. Perhaps the efforts of historians and educators together will help to facilitate the hoped-for "new era in education, rather than a new error."

Index